# Learning Ansible 2

## Second Edition

Learn everything you need to manage and handle your systems with ease with Ansible 2 using this comprehensive guide

Fabio Alessandro Locati

BIRMINGHAM - MUMBAI

# Learning Ansible 2

## Second Edition

Copyright © 2016 Packt Publishing

All rights reserved. No part of this book may be reproduced, stored in a retrieval system, or transmitted in any form or by any means, without the prior written permission of the publisher, except in the case of brief quotations embedded in critical articles or reviews.

Every effort has been made in the preparation of this book to ensure the accuracy of the information presented. However, the information contained in this book is sold without warranty, either express or implied. Neither the author, nor Packt Publishing, and its dealers and distributors will be held liable for any damages caused or alleged to be caused directly or indirectly by this book.

Packt Publishing has endeavored to provide trademark information about all of the companies and products mentioned in this book by the appropriate use of capitals. However, Packt Publishing cannot guarantee the accuracy of this information.

First published: November 2014

Second edition: November 2016

Production reference: 1161116

Published by Packt Publishing Ltd.
Livery Place
35 Livery Street
Birmingham
B3 2PB, UK.
ISBN 978-1-78646-423-1

www.packtpub.com

# Credits

**Authors**
Fabio Alessandro Locati

**Reviewers**
Tim Rupp

**Commissioning Editor**
Pratik Shah

**Acquisition Editor**
Divya Poojari

**Content Development Editor**
Amedh Gemraram Pohad

**Technical Editor**
Vishal Kamal Mewada

**Copy Editor**
Madhusudan Uchil

**Project Coordinator**
Judie Jose

**Proofreader**
Safis Editing

**Indexer**
Pratik Shirodkar

**Graphics**
Kirk D'Penha

**Production Coordinator**
Shantanu N. Zagade

# About the Author

**Fabio Alessandro Locati** is a senior consultant at Red Hat, public speaker, author, and open source contributor. His main areas of expertise are Linux, security, cloud technologies, and automation. With more than 10 years of working experience in the field, he has experience in different IT roles, technologies, and languages.

He has worked for many different companies, starting from a one-man company to huge companies such as Tech Data and Samsung. This has allowed him to consider various technologies from different points of view, helping him develop critical thinking and swiftly understand whether a particular technology is the right fit for a specific project.

Since he is always looking for better technologies, he also tries new technologies to understand their advantages over the old ones as well as their maturity status. One of the most important things he evaluates about a technology is its internal security and the possibility of adding security through configuration or interaction with other technologies.

In his work and to manage his own machines, he has used Ansible since 2013.

He often gives talks about his work, the projects he helps with in his spare time, and his vision of the IT and security worlds. He is the author of the book *OpenStack Cloud Security*, *Packt Publishing*.

In his spare time, he helps out on the Fedora Project as well as Wikimedia and Open Street Map.

You can find more about him on LinkedIn at `https://www.linkedin.com/in/fabiolocati/en` and at `https://fale.io/`.

*I would like to thank my parents, who introduced me to computer science before I was even able to write, and my whole family, who has always been supportive. A special thanks goes to everyone I worked with at Packt Publishing for their hard work and to Tim Rupp for his great feedbacks. Since Ansible is an open source project, I thank all companies that decided to invest into it as well as all people that decided to volunteer their time to the project.*

# About the Reviewer

**Tim Rupp** has been working in various fields of computing for the last 10 years. He has held positions in computer security, software engineering, and, most recently, in the fields of cloud computing and DevOps.

He was first introduced to Ansible while at Rackspace. As part of the cloud engineering team, he made extensive use of the tool to deploy new capacity for the Rackspace public cloud. Since then, he has contributed patches, provided support for, and presented on Ansible topics at local meetups.

Tim is currently a senior software engineer at F5 Networks, where he works on data plane programmability. He is particularly interested in automation and orchestration surrounding F5 products and is the maintainer of the BIG-IP modules in Ansible.

# www.PacktPub.com

For support files and downloads related to your book, please visit www.PacktPub.com.

Did you know that Packt offers eBook versions of every book published, with PDF and ePub files available? You can upgrade to the eBook version at www.PacktPub.com and as a print book customer, you are entitled to a discount on the eBook copy. Get in touch with us at service@packtpub.com for more details.

At www.PacktPub.com, you can also read a collection of free technical articles, sign up for a range of free newsletters and receive exclusive discounts and offers on Packt books and eBooks.

https://www.packtpub.com/mapt

Get the most in-demand software skills with Mapt. Mapt gives you full access to all Packt books and video courses, as well as industry-leading tools to help you plan your personal development and advance your career.

## Why subscribe?

- Fully searchable across every book published by Packt
- Copy and paste, print, and bookmark content
- On demand and accessible via a web browser

# Table of Contents

| | |
|---|---|
| **Preface** | 1 |
| **Chapter 1: Getting Started with Ansible** | 7 |
|     **IT automation** | 8 |
|         The history of IT automation | 8 |
|         Advantages of IT automation | 8 |
|         Disadvantages of IT automation | 9 |
|             Limiting the possible damages of an error propagation | 9 |
|         Types of IT automation | 11 |
|             Agent-based systems | 11 |
|             Agent-less systems | 12 |
|             Agent-based versus Agent-less systems | 12 |
|     **What is Ansible?** | 13 |
|     **Secure Shell (SSH)** | 13 |
|     **Why Ansible?** | 13 |
|     **Installing Ansible** | 14 |
|         Installing Ansible using the system's package manager | 15 |
|             Installing via Yum | 15 |
|             Installing via Apt | 15 |
|             Installing via Homebrew | 15 |
|             Installing via pip | 16 |
|             Installing Ansible from source | 16 |
|     **Creating a test environment with QEMU and KVM** | 18 |
|     **Version control system** | 22 |
|     **Using Ansible with Git** | 24 |
|     **Summary** | 25 |
| **Chapter 2: Automating Simple Tasks** | 27 |
|     **YAML** | 27 |
|     **Hello Ansible** | 28 |
|     **Working with playbooks** | 30 |
|         Studying the anatomy of a playbook | 30 |
|         Running a playbook | 32 |
|     **Ansible verbosity** | 37 |
|     **Variables in playbooks** | 38 |
|     **Creating the Ansible user** | 48 |
|     **Configuring a basic server** | 49 |

|   |   |
|---|---|
| Enabling EPEL | 49 |
| Installing Python bindings for SELinux | 50 |
| Upgrading all installed packages | 50 |
| Ensuring that NTP is installed, configured, and running | 51 |
| Ensuring that FirewallD is present and enabled | 52 |
| Adding a customized MOTD | 53 |
| Changing the hostname | 54 |
| Reviewing and running the playbook | 54 |
| **Installing and configuring a web server** | **57** |
| **Publishing a website** | **58** |
| **Jinja2 templates** | **60** |
| Variables | 60 |
| Filters | 60 |
| Conditionals | 60 |
| Cycles | 61 |
| **Summary** | **62** |
| **Chapter 3: Scaling to Multiple Hosts** | **63** |
| **Working with inventory files** | **63** |
| The basic inventory file | 64 |
| Groups in an inventory file | 64 |
| Regular expressions in the inventory file | 66 |
| **Working with variables** | **66** |
| Host variables | 67 |
| Group variables | 67 |
| Variable files | 68 |
| Overriding configuration parameters with an inventory file | 68 |
| **Working with dynamic inventory** | **69** |
| Amazon Web Services | 70 |
| DigitalOcean | 71 |
| **Working with iterates in Ansible** | **72** |
| Standard iteration – with_items | 73 |
| Nested loops – with_nested | 74 |
| Fileglobs loop – with_fileglobs | 76 |
| Integer loop – with_sequence | 77 |
| **Summary** | **79** |
| **Chapter 4: Handling Complex Deployment** | **81** |
| **Working with the local_action feature** | **82** |
| **Delegating a task** | **83** |

| | |
|---|---|
| **Working with conditionals** | 85 |
| Boolean conditionals | 87 |
| Checking if a variable is set | 89 |
| **Working with include** | 89 |
| **Working with handlers** | 90 |
| **Working with roles** | 93 |
| Project organization | 93 |
| Anatomy of a role | 94 |
| Transforming your playbooks in a full Ansible project | 94 |
|     Transforming a playbook into a role | 95 |
|     Helper files | 98 |
|     Transforming the webserver role | 101 |
|     Handlers in roles | 102 |
| **Execution strategies** | 105 |
| **Tasks blocks** | 106 |
| **The Ansible template – Jinja filters** | 106 |
| Formatting data using filters | 107 |
| Using filters with conditionals | 108 |
| Defaulting undefined variables | 109 |
| **Security management** | 110 |
| Using Ansible vault | 110 |
| Vaults and playbooks | 113 |
| Encrypting user passwords | 114 |
| Hiding passwords | 115 |
| Using no_log | 116 |
| **Summary** | 117 |
| **Chapter 5: Going Cloud** | 119 |
| **Provisioning resources in the cloud** | 120 |
| **Amazon Web Service** | 121 |
| AWS global infrastructure | 122 |
| AWS Simple Storage Service | 122 |
| AWS Elastic Compute Cloud (EC2) | 123 |
| AWS Virtual Private Cloud (VPC) | 123 |
| AWS Route 53 | 124 |
| AWS Elastic Block Storage (EBS) | 124 |
| AWS Identity and Access Management | 125 |
| Amazon relational database service | 125 |
| Setting up an account with AWS | 125 |
| Simple AWS deployment | 127 |

| | |
|---|---|
| Complex AWS deployment | 134 |
| **DigitalOcean** | **135** |
| Droplets | 136 |
| SSH key management | 136 |
| Private networking | 137 |
| Adding an SSH key in DigitalOcean | 137 |
| Deployment in DigitalOcean | 138 |
| **Summary** | **141** |

## Chapter 6: Getting Notifications from Ansible — 143

| | |
|---|---|
| **E-mails** | **144** |
| **XMPP** | **146** |
| **Slack** | **147** |
| **Rocket Chat** | **148** |
| **Internet Relay Chat (IRC)** | **149** |
| **Amazon Simple Notification Service** | **151** |
| **Nagios** | **153** |
| **Summary** | **156** |

## Chapter 7: Creating a Custom Module — 157

| | |
|---|---|
| **Using Python modules** | **159** |
| Working with exit_json and fail_json | 165 |
| Testing Python modules | 167 |
| **Using bash modules** | **168** |
| **Using Ruby modules** | **170** |
| **Testing modules** | **174** |
| **Summary** | **177** |

## Chapter 8: Debugging and Error Handling — 179

| | |
|---|---|
| **The check mode** | **181** |
| **Indicating differences between files using --diff** | **183** |
| **Functional testing in Ansible** | **186** |
| **Functional testing using assert** | **186** |
| **Testing with tags** | **188** |
| **The --skip-tags** | **190** |
| **Managing exceptions** | **190** |
| **Trigger failure** | **194** |
| **Summary** | **195** |

## Chapter 9: Complex Environments — 197

| | |
|---|---|
| **Code based on the Git branch** | **198** |

| | |
|---|---|
| A single stable branch with multiple folders | 198 |
| **Software distribution strategy** | 203 |
|     Copying files from the local machine | 204 |
|     Revision control system with branches | 204 |
|     Revision control system with tags | 205 |
|     RPM packages | 206 |
| **Preparing the environment** | 206 |
| **Deploying a web app with revision control systems** | 211 |
| **Deploying a web app with RPM packages** | 214 |
|     Creating a Spec file | 214 |
|     Building RPMs manually | 217 |
|     Building RPMs with Ansible | 219 |
|     Building RPMs with CI/CD pipelines | 226 |
| **Building compiled software with RPM packaging** | 226 |
| **Deployment strategies** | 231 |
|     Canary deployment | 232 |
|     Blue/Green deployment | 233 |
| **Optimizations** | 234 |
|     Pipelining | 234 |
|     Optimizing with_items | 235 |
|     Understanding what happens when your tasks are executed | 235 |
| **Summary** | 236 |
| **Chapter 10: Introducing Ansible for Enterprises** | **237** |
| **Ansible on Windows** | 237 |
| **Ansible for networking devices** | 239 |
| **Ansible Galaxy** | 240 |
| **Ansible Tower** | 244 |
| **Summary** | 245 |
| **Index** | **247** |

# Preface

The information technology sector is a fast-moving sector that always tries to accelerate. To keep up with this, companies need to be able to move quickly and iterate frequently. Until a few years back, this was mainly true for software, but now we start to see the necessity to change infrastructures at similar speed. Going forward, we will need to change the infrastructure we run our software on at the speed of the software itself.

In this scenario, many technologies, such as software-defined everything (storage, network, compute, what have you), will be key, but those technologies need to be managed in an equally scalable way, and that way will be using Ansible and similar products.

Ansible is highly relevant today since, differently from competing products, it is agentless, allowing faster deployments, more security, and better auditability.

## What this book covers

Chapter 1, *Getting Started with Ansible*, explains how to install Ansible.

Chapter 2, *Automating Simple Tasks*, explains how to create simple playbooks that will allow you to automate some simple tasks that you already perform on a daily basis.

Chapter 3, *Scaling to Multiple Hosts*, explains how to handle multiple hosts in Ansible in an easy-to-scale way.

Chapter 4, *Handling Complex Deployment*, explains how to create deployments that have multiple phases as well as multiple machines.

Chapter 5, *Going Cloud*, explains how Ansible can integrate with various cloud offering and how it can simplify your life, managing the cloud for you.

Chapter 6, *Getting Notifications from Ansible*, explains how to set up Ansible to return valuable information to you and other stakeholders.

Chapter 7, *Creating a Custom Module*, explains how to create a custom module to leverage the freedom Ansible gives you.

Chapter 8, *Debugging and Error Handling*, explains how to debug and test Ansible to ensure that your playbooks will always work.

Chapter 9, *Complex Environments*, explains how to manage multiple tiers, multiple environments, and deployments with Ansible.

Chapter 10, *Introducing Ansible for Enterprises*, explains how to manage Windows nodes from Ansible as well as how to leverage Ansible Galaxy and Ansible Tower to maximize your productivity.

# What you need for this book

This book is written to work with all Linux distributions. Since it's not practical to always give the same information for all possible distributions, the example commands are for Fedora on the controller machine and CentOS on the controlled machines, if not stated. Experienced users with other distributions will have no problem in translating the commands for their own preferred distribution.

# Who this book is for

The book is for developers and sysadmins who want to automate their organization's infrastructure using Ansible 2. No prior knowledge of Ansible is required.

# Conventions

In this book, you will find a number of text styles that distinguish between different kinds of information. Here are some examples of these styles and an explanation of their meaning.

Code words in text, database table names, folder names, filenames, file extensions, pathnames, dummy URLs, user input, and Twitter handles are shown as follows: "The `ec2.py` file will create multiple groups based on the region, availability zone, tags, and so on."

A block of code is set as follows:

```
---
- hosts: all
  remote_user: ansible
  vars:
    users:
    - alice
    - bob
```

```
    folders:
    - mail
    - public_html
```

When we wish to draw your attention to a particular part of a code block, the relevant lines or items are set in bold:

```
---
- hosts: all
  remote_user: ansible
  vars:
    users:
    - alice
    - bob
    folders:
    - mail
    - public_html
```

Any command-line input or output is written as follows:

```
$ ansible-playbook -i test01.fale.io, webserver.yaml
```

**New terms** and **important words** are shown in bold. Words that you see on the screen, for example, in menus or dialog boxes, appear in the text like this: "Clicking the Next button moves you to the next screen."

Warnings or important notes appear in a box like this.

Tips and tricks appear like this.

# Reader feedback

Feedback from our readers is always welcome. Let us know what you think about this book—what you liked or disliked. Reader feedback is important for us as it helps us develop titles that you will really get the most out of.

# Preface

To send us general feedback, simply e-mail `feedback@packtpub.com`, and mention the book's title in the subject of your message.

If there is a topic that you have expertise in and you are interested in either writing or contributing to a book, see our author guide at `www.packtpub.com/authors`.

## Customer support

Now that you are the proud owner of a Packt book, we have a number of things to help you to get the most from your purchase.

## Downloading the example code

You can download the example code files for this book from your account at `http://www.packtpub.com`. If you purchased this book elsewhere, you can visit `http://www.packtpub.com/support` and register to have the files e-mailed directly to you.

You can download the code files by following these steps:

1. Log in or register to our website using your e-mail address and password.
2. Hover the mouse pointer on the **SUPPORT** tab at the top.
3. Click on **Code Downloads & Errata**.
4. Enter the name of the book in the **Search** box.
5. Select the book for which you're looking to download the code files.
6. Choose from the drop-down menu where you purchased this book from.
7. Click on **Code Download**.

You can also download the code files by clicking on the **Code Files** button on the book's webpage at the Packt Publishing website. This page can be accessed by entering the book's name in the **Search box**. Please note that you need to be logged in to your Packt account.

Once the file is downloaded, please make sure that you unzip or extract the folder using the latest version of:

- WinRAR / 7-Zip for Windows
- Zipeg / iZip / UnRarX for Mac
- 7-Zip / PeaZip for Linux

The code bundle for the book is also hosted on GitHub at `https://github.com/PacktPublishing/Learning-Ansible-2-Second-Edition`. We also have other code bundles from our rich catalog of books and videos available at `https://github.com/PacktPublishing/`. Check them out!

# Errata

Although we have taken every care to ensure the accuracy of our content, mistakes do happen. If you find a mistake in one of our books—maybe a mistake in the text or the code—we would be grateful if you could report this to us. By doing so, you can save other readers from frustration and help us improve subsequent versions of this book. If you find any errata, please report them by visiting `http://www.packtpub.com/submit-errata`, selecting your book, clicking on the **Errata Submission Form** link, and entering the details of your errata. Once your errata are verified, your submission will be accepted and the errata will be uploaded to our website or added to any list of existing errata under the Errata section of that title.

To view the previously submitted errata, go to `https://www.packtpub.com/books/content/support` and enter the name of the book in the search field. The required information will appear under the **Errata** section.

# Piracy

Piracy of copyrighted material on the Internet is an ongoing problem across all media. At Packt, we take the protection of our copyright and licenses very seriously. If you come across any illegal copies of our works in any form on the Internet, please provide us with the location address or website name immediately so that we can pursue a remedy.

Please contact us at `copyright@packtpub.com` with a link to the suspected pirated material.

We appreciate your help in protecting our authors and our ability to bring you valuable content.

# Questions

If you have a problem with any aspect of this book, you can contact us at `questions@packtpub.com`, and we will do our best to address the problem.

# 1
# Getting Started with Ansible

ICT is often described as a fast-growing industry. I think the best quality of the ICT industry is not related to its ability to grow at a super high speed, but to its ability to revolutionize itself and the rest of the world at an astonishing speed.

Every 10 to 15 years there are major shifts in how this industry works and every shift solves problems that were very hard to manage up to that point, creating new challenges. Also, at every major shift, many best practices of the previous iteration are classified as anti-patterns and new best practices are created. Although it might appear that those changes are impossible to predict, this is not always true. Obviously, it is not possible to know exactly what changes will occur and when they will take place, but looking at companies with a large number of servers and many lines of code usually reveals what the next steps will be.

The current shift has already happened in big companies like Amazon Web Services, Facebook, and Google. It is the implementation of IT automation systems to create and manage servers.

In this chapter we will cover:

- IT automation
- What is Ansible?
- The secure shell
- Installing Ansible
- Creating a test environment with QEMU and KVM
- Version control system
- Using Ansible with Git

# IT automation

IT automation is in its larger sense—the processes and software that help with the management of the IT infrastructure (servers, networking, and storage). In the current shift, we are assisting to a huge implementation of such processes and software.

## The history of IT automation

At the beginning of IT history, there were very few servers and a lot of people were needed to make them work properly, usually more than one person for each machine. Over the years, servers became more reliable and easier to manage so it was possible to have multiple servers managed by a single system administrator. In that period, the administrators manually installed the software, upgraded the software manually, and changed the configuration files manually. This was obviously a very labor-intensive and error-prone process, so many administrators started to implement scripts and other means to make their life easier. Those scripts were (usually) pretty complex and they did not scale very well.

In the early years of this century, data centers started to grow a lot due to companies' needs. Virtualization helped in keeping prices low and the fact that many of these services were web services, meant that many servers were very similar to each other. At this point, new tools were needed to substitute the scripts that were used before, the configuration management tools.

**CFEngine** was one of the first tools to demonstrate configuration management capabilities way back in the 1990s; more recently, there has been Puppet, Chef, and Salt, besides Ansible.

## Advantages of IT automation

People often wonder if IT automation really brings enough advantages considering that implementing it has some direct and indirect costs. The main advantages of IT automation are:

- Ability to provision machines quickly
- Ability to recreate a machine from scratch in minutes
- Ability to track any change performed on the infrastructure

For these reasons, it's possible to reduce the cost of managing the IT infrastructure by reducing the repetitive operations often performed by system administrators.

# Disadvantages of IT automation

As with any other technology, IT automation does come with some disadvantages. From my point of view these are the biggest disadvantages:

- Automating all of the small tasks that were once used to train new system administrators
- If an error is performed, it will be propagated everywhere

The consequence of the first is that new ways to train junior system administrators will need to be implemented.

## Limiting the possible damages of an error propagation

The second one is trickier. There are a lot of ways to limit this kind of damage, but none of those will prevent it completely. The following mitigation options are available:

- **Always have backups**: Backups will not prevent you from nuking your machine; they will only make the restore process possible.
- **Always test your infrastructure code (playbooks/roles) in a non-production environment**: Companies have developed different pipelines to deploy code and those usually include environments such as dev, test, staging, and production. Use the same pipeline to test your infrastructure code. If a buggy application reaches the production environment it could be a problem. If a buggy playbook reaches the production environment, it could be catastrophic.
- **Always peer-review your infrastructure code**: Some companies have already introduced peer-reviews for the application code, but very few have introduced it for the infrastructure code. As I was saying in the previous point, I think infrastructure code is way more critical than application code, so you should always peer-review your infrastructure code, whether you do it for your application code or not.
- **Enable SELinux**: SELinux is a security kernel module that is available on all Linux distributions (it is installed by default on Fedora, Red Hat Enterprise Linux, CentOS, Scientific Linux, and Unbreakable Linux). It allows you to limit users and process powers in a very granular way. I suggest using SELinux instead of other similar modules (such as AppArmor) because it is able to handle more situations and permissions. SELinux will prevent a huge amount of damage because, if correctly configured, it will prevent many dangerous commands from being executed.

- **Run the playbooks from a limited account**: Even though user and privilege escalation schemes have been in UNIX code for more than 40 years, it seems as if not many companies use them. Using a limited user for all your playbooks, and escalating privileges only for commands that need higher privileges will help prevent you nuking a machine while trying to clean an application temporary folder.
- **Use horizontal privilege escalation**: The `sudo` is a well-known command but is often used in its more dangerous form. The `sudo` command supports the '-u' parameter that will allow you to specify a user that you want to impersonate. If you have to change a file that is owned by another user, please do not escalate to `root` to do so, just escalate to that user. In Ansible, you can use the `become_user` parameter to achieve this.
- **When possible, don't run a playbook on all your machines at the same time**: Staged deployments can help you detect a problem before it's too late. There are many problems that are not detectable in a dev, test, staging, and qa environment. The majority of them are related to load that is hard to emulate properly in those non-production environments. A new configuration you have just added to your Apache HTTPd or MySQL servers could be perfectly OK from a syntax point of view, but disastrous for your specific application under your production load. A staged deployment will allow you to test your new configuration on your actual load without risking downtime if something was wrong.
- **Avoid guessing commands and modifiers**: A lot of system administrators will try to remember the right parameter and try to guess if they don't remember it exactly. I've done it too, a lot of times, but this is very risky. Checking the man page or the online documentation will usually take you less than two minutes and often, by reading the manual, you'll find interesting notes you did not know. Guessing modifiers is dangerous because you could be fooled by a non-standard modifier (that is, `-v` is not the verbose mode for `grep` and `-h` is not the `help` command for the MySQL CLI).
- **Avoid error-prone commands**: Not all commands have been created equally. Some commands are (way) more dangerous than others. If you can assume a `cat` command safe, you have to assume that a `dd` command is dangerous, since `dd` perform copies and conversion of files and volumes. I've seen people using `dd` in scripts to transform DOS files to UNIX (instead of `dos2unix`) and many other, very dangerous, examples. Please, avoid such commands, because they could result in a huge disaster if something goes wrong.

- **Avoid unnecessary modifiers**: If you need to delete a simple file, use `rm ${file}` not `rm -rf ${file}`. The latter is often performed by users that have learned that; "to be sure, always use `rm -rf`", because at some time in their past, they have had to delete a folder. This will prevent you from deleting an entire folder if the `${file}` variable is set wrongly.
- **Always check what could happen if a variable is not set**: If you want to delete the contents of a folder and you use the `rm -rf ${folder}/*` command, you are looking for trouble. If the `${folder}` variable is not set for some reason, the shell will read a `rm -rf /*` command, which is deadly (considering the fact that the `rm -rf /` command will not work on the majority of current OSes because it requires a `--no-preserve-root` option, while `rm -rf /*` will work as expected). I'm using this specific command as an example because I have seen such situations: the variable was pulled from a database which, due to some maintenance work, was down and an empty string was assigned to that variable. What happened next is probably easy to guess. In case you cannot prevent using variables in dangerous places, at least check them to see if they are not empty before using them. This will not save you from every problem but may catch some of the most common ones.
- **Double check your redirections**: Redirections (along with pipes) are the most powerful elements of Linux shells. They could also be very dangerous: a `cat /dev/rand > /dev/sda` command can destroy a disk even if a `cat` command is usually overlooked because it's not usually dangerous. Always double-check all commands that include a redirection.
- **Use specific modules wherever possible**: In this list I've used shell commands because many people will try to use Ansible as if it's just a way to distribute them: it's not. Ansible provides a lot of modules and we'll see them in this book. They will help you create more readable, portable, and safe playbooks.

# Types of IT automation

There are a lot of ways to classify IT automation systems, but by far the most important is related to how the configurations are propagated. Based on this, we can distinguish between agent-based systems and agent-less systems.

## Agent-based systems

Agent-based systems have two different components: a **server** and a client called **agent**.

There is only one server and it contains all of the configuration for your whole environment, while the agents are as many as the machines in the environment.

 In some cases, more than one server could be present to ensure high availability, but treat it as if it's a single server, since they will all be configured in the same way.

Periodically, client will contact the server to see if a new configuration for its machine is present. If a new configuration is present, the client will download it and apply it.

## Agent-less systems

In agent-less systems, no specific agent is present. Agent-less systems do not always respect the server/client paradigm, since it's possible to have multiple servers and even the same number of servers and clients . Communications are initialized by the server that will contact the client(s) using standard protocols (usually via SSH and PowerShell).

## Agent-based versus Agent-less systems

Aside from the differences outlined above, there are other contrasting factors which arise because of those differences.

From a security standpoint, an agent-based system can be less secure. Since all machines have to be able to initiate a connection to the server machine, this machine could be attacked more easily than in an agent-less case where the machine is usually behind a firewall that will not accept any incoming connections.

From a performance point of view, agent-based systems run the risk of having the server saturated and therefore the roll-out could be slower. It also needs to be considered that, in a pure agent-based system, it is not possible to force-push an update immediately to a set of machines. It will have to wait until those machines check-in. For this reason, multiple agent-based systems have implemented out-of-bands wait to implement such feature. Tools such as Chef and Puppet are agent-based but can also run without a centralized server to scale a large number of machines, commonly called **Serverless Chef** and **Masterless Puppet**, respectively.

An agent-less system is easier to integrate in an infrastructure that is already present, since it will be seen by the clients as a normal SSH connection and therefore no additional configuration is needed.

# What is Ansible?

Ansible is an agent-less IT automation tool developed in 2012 by *Michael DeHaan*, a former Red Hat associate. The Ansible design goals are for it to be: minimal, consistent, secure, highly reliable, and easy to learn. The Ansible company has recently been bought out by Red Hat and now operates as part of Red Hat, Inc.

Ansible primarily runs in push mode using SSH, but you can also run Ansible using `ansible-pull`, where you can install Ansible on each agent, download the playbooks locally, and run them on individual machines. If there is a large number of machines (large is a relative term; in our view, greater than 500 and requiring parallel updates), and you plan to deploy updates to the machines in parallel, this might be the right way to go about it.

# Secure Shell (SSH)

**Secure Shell** (also known as **SSH**) is a network service that allows you to login and access a shell remotely in a fully encrypted connection. The SSH daemon is today, the standard for UNIX system administration, after having replaced the unencrypted telnet. The most frequently used implementation of the SSH protocol is OpenSSH.

In the last few months, Microsoft has shown an implementation (at the time of writing) of OpenSSH for Windows.

Since Ansible performs SSH connections and commands in the same way any other SSH client would do, no specific configuration has been applied to the OpenSSH server.

To speed up default SSH connections, you can always enable `ControlPersist` and the pipeline mode, which makes Ansible faster and secure.

# Why Ansible?

We will try and compare Ansible with Puppet and Chef during the course of this book since many people have good experience with those tools. We will also point out specifically how Ansible would solve a problem compared to Chef or Puppet.

Ansible, as well as Puppet and Chef, are declarative in nature and are expected to move a machine to the desired state specified in the configuration. For example, in each of these tools, in order to start a service at a point in time and start it automatically on restart, you would need to write a declarative block or module; every time the tool runs on the machine, it will aspire to obtain the state defined in your **playbook** (Ansible), **cookbook** (Chef), or **manifest** (Puppet).

The difference in the toolset is minimal at a simple level but as more situations arise and the complexity increases, you will start finding differences between the different toolsets. In Puppet, you need to take care of the order, and the Puppet server will create the sequence of instructions to execute every time you run it on a different box. To exploit the power of Chef, you will need a good Ruby team. Your team needs to be good at the Ruby language to customize both Puppet and Chef, and there will be a bigger learning curve with both of the tools.

With Ansible, the case is different. It uses the simplicity of Chef when it comes to the order of execution, the top-to-bottom approach, and allows you to define the end state in YAML format, which makes the code extremely readable and easy for everyone, from development teams to operations teams, to pick up and make changes. In many cases, even without Ansible, operations teams are given playbook manuals to execute instructions from, whenever they face issues. Ansible mimics that behavior. Do not be surprised if you end up having your project manager change the code in Ansible and check it into Git because of its simplicity!

## Installing Ansible

Installing Ansible is rather quick and simple. You can use the source code directly, by cloning it from the GitHub project (`https://github.com/ansible/ansible`), install it using your system's package manager, or use Python's package management tool (**pip**). You can use Ansible on any Windows, Mac, or UNIX-like system. Ansible doesn't require any databases and doesn't need any daemons running. This makes it easier to maintain Ansible versions and upgrade without any breaks.

We'd like to call the machine where we will install Ansible our Ansible workstation. Some people also refer to it as the command center.

# Installing Ansible using the system's package manager

It is possible to install Ansible using the system's package manager and in my opinion this is the preferred option if your system's package manager ships at least Ansible 2.0. We will look into installing Ansible via **Yum**, **Apt**, **Homebrew**, and **pip**.

## Installing via Yum

If you are running a Fedora system you can install Ansible directly, since from Fedora 22, Ansible 2.0+ is available in the official repositories. You can install it as follows:

    $ sudo dnf install ansible

For RHEL and RHEL-based (CentOS, Scientific Linux, Unbreakable Linux) systems, versions 6 and 7 have Ansible 2.0+ available in the EPEL repository, so you should ensure that you have the EPEL repository enabled before installing Ansible as follows:

    $ sudo yum install ansible

> On Cent 6 or RHEL 6, you have to run the command `rpm -Uvh`. Refer to `http://dl.fedoraproject.org/pub/epel/6/x86_64/epel-release-6-8.noarch.rpm` for instructions on how to install EPEL.

## Installing via Apt

Ansible is available for Ubuntu and Debian. To install Ansible on those operating systems, use the following command:

    $ sudo apt-get install ansible

## Installing via Homebrew

You can install Ansible on Mac OS X using Homebrew, as follows:

    $ brew update
    $ brew install ansible

## Installing via pip

You can install Ansible via pip. If you don't have pip installed on your system, install it. You can use pip to install Ansible on Windows too, using the following command line:

```
$ sudo easy_install pip
```

You can now install Ansible using `pip`, as follows:

```
$ sudo pip install ansible
```

Once you're done installing Ansible, run `ansible --version` to verify that it has been installed:

```
$ ansible --version
```

You will get the following output from the preceding command line:

```
ansible 2.0.2
```

## Installing Ansible from source

In case the previous methods do not fit your use case, you can install Ansible directly from the source. Installing from source does not require any root permissions. Let's clone a repository and activate `virtualenv`, which is an isolated environment in Python where you can install packages without interfering with the system's Python packages. The command and the resulting output for the repository is as follows:

```
$ git clone git://github.com/ansible/ansible.git
Cloning into 'ansible'...
remote: Counting objects: 116403, done.
remote: Compressing objects: 100% (18/18), done.
remote: Total 116403 (delta 3), reused 0 (delta 0), pack-reused 116384
Receiving objects: 100% (116403/116403), 40.80 MiB | 844.00 KiB/s, done.
Resolving deltas: 100% (69450/69450), done.
Checking connectivity... done.
$ cd ansible/
$ source ./hacking/env-setup
Setting up Ansible to run out of checkout...
PATH=/home/vagrant/ansible/bin:/usr/local/bin:/bin:/usr/bin:/usr/local/sbin:/usr/sbin:/sbin:/home/vagrant/bin
PYTHONPATH=/home/vagrant/ansible/lib:
MANPATH=/home/vagrant/ansible/docs/man:
Remember, you may wish to specify your host file with -i
Done!
```

*Chapter 1*

Ansible needs a couple of Python packages, which you can install using `pip`. If you don't have pip installed on your system, install it using the following command. If you don't have `easy_install` installed, you can install it using Python's `setuptools` package on Red Hat systems, or by using Brew on the Mac:

```
$ sudo easy_install pip
<A long output follows>
```

Once you have installed `pip`, install the `paramiko`, `PyYAML`, `jinja2`, and `httplib2` packages using the following command lines:

```
$ sudo pip install paramiko PyYAML jinja2 httplib2
    Requirement already satisfied (use --upgrade to upgrade): paramiko in /usr/lib/python2.6/site-packages
    Requirement already satisfied (use --upgrade to upgrade): PyYAML in /usr/lib64/python2.6/site-packages
    Requirement already satisfied (use --upgrade to upgrade): jinja2 in /usr/lib/python2.6/site-packages
    Requirement already satisfied (use --upgrade to upgrade): httplib2 in /usr/lib/python2.6/site-packages
    Downloading/unpacking markupsafe (from jinja2)
      Downloading MarkupSafe-0.23.tar.gz
      Running setup.py (path:/tmp/pip_build_root/markupsafe/setup.py) egg_info for package markupsafe
    Installing collected packages: markupsafe
      Running setup.py install for markupsafe
        building 'markupsafe._speedups' extension
        gcc -pthread -fno-strict-aliasing -O2 -g -pipe -Wall -Wp,-D_FORTIFY_SOURCE=2 -fexceptions -fstack-protector --param=ssp-buffer-size=4 -m64 -mtune=generic -D_GNU_SOURCE -fPIC -fwrapv -DNDEBUG -O2 -g -pipe -Wall -Wp,-D_FORTIFY_SOURCE=2 -fexceptions -fstack-protector --param=ssp-buffer-size=4 -m64 -mtune=generic -D_GNU_SOURCE -fPIC -fwrapv -fPIC -I/usr/include/python2.6 -c markupsafe/_speedups.c -o build/temp.linux-x86_64-2.6/markupsafe/_speedups.o
        gcc -pthread -shared build/temp.linux-x86_64-2.6/markupsafe/_speedups.o -L/usr/lib64 -lpython2.6 -o build/lib.linux-x86_64-2.6/markupsafe/_speedups.so
    Successfully installed markupsafe
    Cleaning up...
```

> By default, Ansible will be running against the development branch. You might want to check out the latest stable branch. Check what the latest stable version is using the following command line:
> **$ git branch -a**

*Getting Started with Ansible*

Copy the latest version you want to use. Version 2.0.2 was the latest version available at the time of writing. Check the latest version using the following command lines:

```
[node ansible]$ git checkout v2.0.2
Note: checking out 'v2.0.2'.
[node ansible]$ ansible --version
ansible 2.0.2 (v2.0.2 268e72318f) last updated 2014/09/28 21:27:25 (GMT +000)
```

You now have a working setup of Ansible ready. One of the benefits of running Ansible from source is that you can enjoy the new features immediately, without waiting for your package manager to make them available for you.

# Creating a test environment with QEMU and KVM

To be able to learn Ansible, we will need to make quite a few playbooks and run them.

> Doing it directly on your computer will be very risky. For this reason, I would suggest using virtual machines.

It's possible to create a test environment with cloud providers in a few seconds, but often it is more useful to have those machines locally. To do so, we will use **Kernel-based Virtual Machine** (**KVM**) with **Quick Emulator** (**QEMU**).

The first thing will be installing `qemu-kvm` and `virt-install`. On Fedora it will be enough to run:

```
$ sudo dnf install -y @virtualization
```

On Red Hat/CentOS/Scientific Linux/Unbreakable Linux it will be enough to run:

```
$ sudo yum install -y qemu-kvm virt-install virt-manager
```

If you use Ubuntu, you can install it using:

```
$ sudo apt install virt-manager
```

On Debian, you'll need to execute:

```
$ sudo apt install qemu-kvm libvirt-bin
```

For our examples, I'll be using CentOS 7. This is for multiple reasons; the main ones are:

- CentOS is free and 100% compatible with Red Hat, Scientific Linux, and Unbreakable Linux
- Many companies use Red Hat/CentOS/Scientific Linux/Unbreakable Linux for their servers
- Those distributions are the only ones with SELinux support built in, and as we have seen earlier, SELinux can help you make your environment much more secure

At the time of writing this book, the most recent CentOS cloud image is http://cloud.centos.org/centos/7/images/CentOS-7-x86_64-GenericCloud-1603.qcow2, So let's download this image with the help of the following command:

```
$ wget http://cloud.centos.org/centos/7/images/CentOS-7-x86_64-GenericCloud-1603.qcow2
```

Since we will probably need to create many machines, it's better if we create a copy of it so the original one will not be modified:

```
$ cp CentOS-7-x86_64-GenericCloud-1603.qcow2 centos_1.qcow2
```

Since the `qcow2` images will run `cloud-init` to set up the networking, users, and so on, we will need to provide a couple of files. Let's start by creating a metadata file for networking:

```
instance-id: centos_1
local-hostname: centos_1.local
network-interfaces: |
  iface eth0 inet static
  address (An IP in your virtual bridge class)
  network (The first IP of the virtual bridge class)
  netmask (Your virtual bridge class netmask)
  broadcast (Your virtual bridge class broadcast)
  gateway (Your virtual bridge class gateway)
```

To find your virtual bridge data, you have to look for a device that has the name `virbrX` or something similar, in my case it is `virtbr0`, so I can find all of its information using the following command:

```
$ ip addr show virbr0
```

The previous command will give this as an output:

```
5: virbr0: <NO-CARRIER,BROADCAST,MULTICAST,UP> mtu 1500 qdisc noqueue state DOWN group default qlen 1000
```

*Getting Started with Ansible*

```
link/ether 52:54:00:38:1a:e6 brd ff:ff:ff:ff:ff:ff
inet 192.168.124.1/24 brd 192.168.124.255 scope global virbr0
   valid_lft forever preferred_lft forever
```

So, for me the meta-data file looks like the following:

```
instance-id: centos_1
local-hostname: centos_1.local
network-interfaces: |
  iface eth0 inet static
  address 192.168.124.10
  network 192.168.124.1
  netmask 255.255.255.0
  broadcast 192.168.124.255
  gateway 192.168.124.1
```

This file will set up the eth0 interface of the virtual machine at boot time. We also need another file (user-data) to set up the users properly:

```
users:
- name: (yourname)
  shell: /bin/bash
  sudo: ['ALL=(ALL) NOPASSWD:ALL']
  ssh-authorized-keys:
  - (insert ssh public key here)
```

For me, the file looks like the following:

```
users:
- name: fale
  shell: /bin/bash
  sudo: ['ALL=(ALL) NOPASSWD:ALL']
  ssh-authorized-keys:
  - ssh-rsa
AAAAB3NzaC1yc2EAAAADAQABAAACAQDRoZzfNif+wXFqzsmvHg4jJt8+ZO/dQxm5k7pXYAwdWVb
iFrZYGhMQl5FPfzC7rkDaC31fod3Y85QkQVgNKCVYUy5QR5LfxUjSQDv+y2Nfao4be/BKla0ffc
7JVSzFFAELGGDLn11MN0e0D9syqQbKgSRdOdvweq/0Et3KNIF9e7XgEdSuAHls17NDtMkWUfyi5
yvEtdtMcp9gO4OlG6Vh0iCXOdx+f0QA2hh1JnvePvzJ4a8CeckN5JwL7Q027nlsHPBYq9K1jvv+
diUs48FflPJI4fgMq3Zo7zyCpf8qE7D1x+u7OvR5kxNdrpnOsDgHeAGNkrzfcmxU7kbU29NX4VF
gWd0sdlzu1nOWFEH7Cnd547tx5VFxBzJwEAUCh7QSiU2Ne/hCnjFkZuDZ5pN4pNw+yu+Feoz79g
V/utoLHuCodYyAvSQlQ7VSfC+djLD/9wHC2yGksvc9ICnSUv3JyQEEEG4K26z6szF9+a3vU0qIq
7YYa8QHgWIHtzSxztYRIWJOzTZlwyuNmhbRNYDaMC5BMzvQ8JREv0obMLmrlvolJPWT4gn1N9sD
NNXIC6RDRE5yGsIEf0CliYW1X/8XG40U+g9LG+lrYOGWD4OymZ2P/VDIzZbVT6NG/rdSSGnf4D1
AwlOGR7eNTv30AK9o0LVjqGaJWKWYUF9zY6I3+Q==
```

To provide those files at boot time, we will need to create an ISO file containing them:

```
$ genisoimage -output centos_1.iso -volid cidata -joliet -rock user-data meta-data
```

After the ISO file is ready, we can instruct `virt-install` to actually create the virtual machine:

```
virt-install --name CentOS_1 \
--ram 2048 \
--disk centos_1.qcow2 \
--vcpus 2 \
--os-variant fedora21 \
--connect qemu:///system \
--network bridge:br0,model=virtio \
--cdrom centos_1.iso \
--boot hd
virt-install --name CentOS_1 \ --ram 2048 \ --disk centos_1.qcow2 \ --vcpus 2 \ --os-variant fedora21 \ --connect qemu:///system \ --network bridge:br0,model=virtio \ --cdrom centos_1.iso \ --boot hd
```

Since our network configuration is in the ISO file, we will need it at every boot. Sadly, by default this does not happen, so we will need to do a few more steps. Firstly, run `virsh`:

```
$ virsh
```

At this point, a `virsh` shell should appear with an output like the following:

```
Welcome to virsh, the virtualization interactive terminal.
Type:  'help' for help with commands
       'quit' to quit
virsh #
```

This means that we switched from bash (or your shell, if you are not using bash) to the virtualization shell. Issue the following command:

```
virsh # edit CentOS_1
```

By doing this we will be able to tweak the configuration of the `CentOS_1` machine. In the disk section, you'll need to find the `cdrom` device that should look like this:

```
<disk type='block' device='cdrom'>
  <driver name='qemu' type='raw'/>
  <target dev='hda' bus='ide'/>
  <readonly/>
  <address type='drive' controller='0' bus='0' target='0' unit='0'/>
</disk>
```

You'll need to change it to the following as highlighted in bold:

```
<disk type='file' device='cdrom'>
  <driver name='qemu' type='raw'/>
    <source file='(Put here your ISO path)/centos_1.iso'/>
  <target dev='hda' bus='ide'/>
  <readonly/>
  <address type='drive' controller='0' bus='0' target='0'
  unit='0'/>
</disk>
```

At this point, our virtual machine will always start with the ISO file mounted as a `cdrom` and therefore `cloud-init` will be able to correctly initiate the networking.

# Version control system

In this chapter, we have already encountered the expression *infrastructure code* to describe the Ansible code that will create and maintain your infrastructure. We use the expression infrastructure code to distinguish it from the application code, which is the code that composes your applications, websites, and so on. This distinction is needed for clarity, but in the end, both types are a bunch of text files that the software will be able to read and interpret.

For this reason, a version control system will help you a lot. Its main advantages are:

- Ability to have multiple people working simultaneously on the same project.
- Ability to perform code reviews in a simple way.
- Ability to have multiple branches for multiple environments (that is, dev, test, qa, staging, and production).
- Ability to track a change so we know when it was introduced, and who introduced it. This makes it easier to understand why that piece of code is there, years (or months) later.

Those advantages are provided to you by the majority of version control systems out there.

Version control systems can be divided into three major groups based on the three different models that they can implement:

- Local data model
- Client-server model
- Distributed model

The first category, the local data model, is the oldest (circa 1972) approach and is used for very specific use cases. This model requires all users to share the same filesystem. Famous examples of it are the **Revision Control System** (**RCS**) and **Source Code Control System** (**SCCS**).

The second category, the client-server model, arrived later (circa 1990) and tried to solve the limitations of the local data model, creating a server that respected the local data model and a set of clients that dealt with the server instead of with the repository itself. This additional layer allowed multiple developers to use local files and synchronize them with a centralized server. Famous examples of this approach are Apache **Subversion** (**SVN**), and **Concurrent Versions System** (**CVS**).

The third category, the distributed model, arrived at the beginning of the twenty-first century and tried to solve the limitations of the client-server model. In fact, in the client-server mode, you could work on the code offline, but you needed to be *online* to commit the changes. The distributed model allows you to handle everything on your local repository (like the local data model), and to merge different repositories on different machines in an easy way. In this new model, it's possible to perform all actions as in the client-server model, with the added benefits of being able to work completely offline as well as the ability to merge changes between peers without passing by the centralized server. Examples of this model are BitKeeper (proprietary software), Git, GNU Bazaar, and Mercurial.

There are some additional advantages that will be provided by only the distributed model, such as:

- Possibility of making commits, browsing history, and performing any other action even if the server is not available
- Easier management of multiple branches for different environments

When it comes to infrastructure code, we have to consider that, frequently, the infrastructure that retains and manages your infrastructure code is kept in the infrastructure code itself. This is a recursive situation that can create problems. In fact, until you have your code server in place you cannot deploy your Ansible, and until you have your Ansible in place, you cannot deploy your code server. A distributed version control system will prevent this problem.

As for the simplicity of managing multiple branches, even if this is not a hard rule, often distributed version control systems have much better merge handling than the other kinds of version control systems.

# Using Ansible with Git

For the reasons that we have just seen and because of its huge popularity, I suggest always using Git for your Ansible repositories.

There are a few suggestions that I always provide to the people I talk to, so Ansible gets the best out of Git:

- **Create environment branches**: Creating environment branches such as dev, prod, test, and stg, will allow you to easily keep track of the different environments and their respective update statuses. I often suggest keeping the master branch for the development environment, since I find many people are used to pushing new changes directly to the master. If you use a master for a production environment, people can inadvertently push changes in the production environment while they wanted to push them in a development environment.
- **Always keep environment branches stable**: One of the big advantages of having environment branches is the possibility of destroying and recreating any environment from scratch at any given moment. This is only possible if your environment branches are in a stable (not broken) state.
- **Use feature branches**: Using different branches for specific long-development features (such as a refactor or some other big changes) will allow you to keep your day-to-day operations while your new feature is in the Git repository (so you'll not lose track of who did what and when they did it).
- **Push often**: I always suggest that people *push commits* as often as possible. This will make Git work as both a version control system and a backup system. I have seen laptops broken, lost, or stolen with days or weeks of unpushed work on them far too often. Don't waste your time, push often. Also, by pushing often, you'll detect merge conflicts sooner, and conflicts are always easier to handle when they are detected early, instead of waiting for multiple changes.
- **Always deploy after you have made a change**: I have seen times when a developer has created a change in the infrastructure code, tested in the dev and test environments, pushed to the production branch, and then went to have lunch before deploying the changes in production. His lunch did not end well. One of his colleagues deployed the code to production inadvertently (he was trying to deploy a small change he had made in the meantime) and was not prepared to handle the other developer's deployment. The production infrastructure broke and they lost a lot of time figuring out how it was possible that such a small change (the one the person who made the deployment was aware of) created such a big mess.

- **Choose multiple small changes rather than a few huge changes**: Making small changes, whenever possible, will make debugging easier. Debugging an infrastructure is not very easy. There is no compiler that will allow you to see *obvious problems* (even though Ansible performs a syntax check of your code, no other test is performed), and the tools for finding something that is broken are not always as good as you would imagine. The infrastructure as a code paradigm is new and tools are not yet as good as the ones for the application code.
- **Avoid binary files as much as possible**: I always suggest keeping your binaries outside your Git repository, whether it is an application code repository or an infrastructure code repository. In the application code example, I think it is important to keep your repository light (Git as well as the majority of the version control systems, do not perform very well with binary blobs), while for the infrastructure code example, it is vital because you'll be tempted to put a huge number of binary blobs in it, since very often it is easier to put a binary blob in the repository than to find a cleaner (and better) solution.

# Summary

In this chapter, we have seen what IT automation is, it's advantages, disadvantages, what kind of tools you can find, and how Ansible fits into this big picture. We have also seen how to install Ansible and how to create a KVM-based virtual machine. In the end, we analyzed the version control systems and spoke about the advantages Git brings to Ansible if used properly.

In the next chapter, we will start looking at the infrastructure code that we mentioned in this chapter without explaining exactly what it is and how to write it. Also in the next chapter, we'll see how to automate simple operations that you probably perform every single day, such as managing users, managing files, and file content.

# 2
# Automating Simple Tasks

As we have mentioned in the previous chapter, Ansible can be used for both, creating and managing a whole infrastructure, as well as be integrated into an infrastructure that is already working.

In this chapter, we will see:

- What a playbook is and how it works
- How to create a web server using Ansible
- A close look at the Jinja2 template engine

But first we will talk about **YAML Ain't Markup Language** (**YAML**), a human-readable data serialization language that is widely used in Ansible.

## YAML

YAML, like many other data serialization languages (such as JSON), has very few, basic concepts:

- Declarations
- Lists
- Associative arrays

A declaration is very similar to a variable in any other language, that is:

```
name: 'This is the name'
```

*Automating Simple Tasks*

To create a list, we will have to use '-':

```
- 'item1'
- 'item2'
- 'item3'
```

YAML uses indentation to logically divide parents from children. So if we want to create associative arrays (also known as objects), we would just need to add an indentation:

```
item:
  name: TheName
  location: TheLocation
```

Obviously, we can mix those together, that is:

```
people:
  - name: Albert
    number: +1000000000
    country: USA
  - name: David
    number: +44000000000
    country: UK
```

Those are the basics of YAML. YAML can do much more, but for now this will be enough.

# Hello Ansible

As we have seen in the previous chapter, it is possible to use Ansible to automate simple tasks that you probably already perform daily.

Let's start by checking if a remote machine is reachable; in other words, let's start by pinging a machine. The simplest way to do this, is to run the following:

```
$ ansible all -i HOST, -m ping
```

Here, `HOST` is an IP address, the **Fully Qualified Domain Name** (**FQDN**), or an alias of a machine where you have SSH access (you can use a **Kernel-based Virtual Machine** (**KVM**), as we have seen in the previous chapter).

 After the "`HOST,`" the comma is mandatory, because otherwise it would not be seen as a list, but as a string.

In this case, we have performed it against a virtual machine on our system:

```
$ ansible all -i test01.fale.io, -m ping
```

You should receive something like this as a result:

```
test01.fale.io | SUCCESS => {
    "changed": false,
    "ping": "pong"
}
```

Now, let's see what we did and why. Let's start from the Ansible help. To query it, we can use the following command:

```
$ ansible --help
```

To make it easier to be read, we have removed all the output related to options that we have not used:

```
Usage: ansible <host-pattern> [options]
Options:
  -i INVENTORY, --inventory-file=INVENTORY
                        specify inventory host path
                        (default=/etc/ansible/hosts) or comma
                        separated host list.
  -m MODULE_NAME, --module-name=MODULE_NAME
                        module name to execute (default=command)
```

So, what we did was:

1. We invoked Ansible.
2. We instructed Ansible to run on all hosts.
3. We specified our inventory (also known as the list of the hosts).
4. We specified the module we wanted to run (`ping`).

Now that we can ping the server, let's `echo hello ansible!`

```
$ ansible all -i test01.fale.io, -m shell -a '/bin/echo hello ansible!'
```

You should receive something like this as a result:

```
test01.fale.io | SUCCESS | rc=0 >>
hello ansible!
```

*Automating Simple Tasks*

In this example, we used an additional option. Let's check the help to see what it does:

```
Usage: ansible <host-pattern> [options]
Options:
  -a MODULE_ARGS, --args=MODULE_ARGS
                        module arguments
```

As you may have guessed from the context and the name, the `args` options allow you to pass additional arguments to the module. Some modules (like `ping`) do not support any arguments, while others (such as `shell`) will require arguments.

# Working with playbooks

Playbooks are one of the core features of Ansible and tell Ansible what to execute. They are like a to-do list for Ansible that contains a list of tasks; each task internally links to a piece of code called a **module**. Playbooks are simple, human-readable YAML files, whereas modules are a piece of code that can be written in any language with the condition that its output be in the JSON format. You can have multiple tasks listed in a playbook and these tasks would be executed serially by Ansible. You can think of playbooks as an equivalent of manifests in Puppet, states in Salt, or cookbooks in Chef; they allow you to enter a list of tasks or commands you want to execute on your remote system.

# Studying the anatomy of a playbook

Playbooks can have a list of remote hosts, user variables, tasks, handlers, and so on. You can also override most of the configuration settings through a playbook. Let's start looking at the anatomy of a playbook.

The purpose of the playbook we are going to consider now, is to ensure that the `httpd` package is installed and the service is **enabled** and **started**. This is the content of the `setup_apache.yaml` file:

```
---
- hosts: all
  remote_user: fale
  tasks:
  - name: Ensure the HTTPd package is installed
    yum:
      name: httpd
      state: present
    become: True
  - name: Ensure the HTTPd service is enabled and running
```

```
    service:
      name: httpd
      state: started
      enabled: True
  become: True
```

The `setup_apache.yaml` file is an example of a playbook. The file is comprised of three main parts, as follows:

- `hosts`: This lists the host or host group against which we want to run the task. The hosts field is mandatory and every playbook should have it. It tells Ansible on which hosts to run the listed tasks. When provided with a host group, Ansible will take the host group from the playbook and try look for it in an inventory file . If there is no match, Ansible will skip all the tasks for that host group. The `--list-hosts` option along with the playbook (`ansible-playbook <playbook> --list-hosts`) will tell you exactly which hosts the playbook will run against.
- `remote_user`: This is one of the configuration parameters of Ansible (consider, for example, `tom -remote_user`) that tells Ansible to use a particular user (in this case, `tom`) while logging into the system.
- `tasks`: Finally, we come to tasks. All playbooks should contain tasks. Tasks are a list of actions you want to perform. A tasks field contains the name of the task (that is, the help text for the user about the task), a module that should be executed, and arguments that are required for the module. Let's look at the single task that is listed in the playbook, as shown in the preceding snippet of code:

 All examples in the book would be executed on CentOS, but the same set of examples with a few changes would work on other distributions as well.

In the preceding case, there are two tasks. The `name` parameter represents what the task is doing and is `present` mainly to improve readability, as we'll see during the playbook run. The `name` parameter is optional. The `modules`, `yum` and `service`, have their own set of parameters. Almost all modules have the `name` parameter (there are exceptions such as the `debug` module), which indicates what component the actions are performed on. Let's look at the other parameters:

- In the `yum` module's case, the `state` parameter has the latest value and it indicates that the `httpd` latest package should be installed. The command to execute more or less translates to `yum install httpd`.

*Automating Simple Tasks*

- In the `service` module's scenario, the `state` parameter with the started value indicates that the `httpd` service should be started, and it roughly translates to `/etc/init.d/httpd` start. In this module we also have the "`enabled`" parameter that defines whether the service should start at boot or not.
- The `become: True` parameter represents the fact that the tasks should be executed with `sudo` access. If the `sudo` user's file does not allow the user to run the particular command, then the playbook will fail when it is run.

> You might have questions about why there is no package module that figures out the architecture internally and runs the `yum`, `apt`, or any other package options depending on the architecture of the system. Ansible populates the package manager value into a variable named `ansible_pkg_manager`.
>
> In general, we need to remember that the number of packages that have a common name across different operating systems is a small subset of the number of packages that are actually present. For example, the `httpd package` is called `httpd` in Red Hat systems and `apache2` in Debian-based systems. We also need to remember that every package manager has its own set of options that make it powerful; as a result, it makes more sense to use explicit package manager names so that the full set of options are available to the end user writing the playbook.

## Running a playbook

Now, it's time (yes, finally!) to run the playbook. To instruct Ansible to execute a playbook instead of a module, we will have to use a different command (`ansible-playbooks`) that has a syntax very similar to the "`ansible`" command we already saw:

```
$ ansible-playbook -i HOST, setup_apache.yaml
```

As you can see, aside from the host-pattern (that is specified in the playbook) that has disappeared, and the module option that has been replaced by the playbook name, nothing changed. So to execute this command on my machine, the exact command is:

```
$ ansible-playbook -i test01.fale.io, setup_apache.yaml
```

The result is the following:

```
PLAY [all] ***********************************************************
TASK [setup] *********************************************************
ok: [test01.fale.io]

TASK [Ensure the HTTPd package is installed] *********************
changed: [test01.fale.io]

TASK [Ensure the HTTPd service is enabled and running] **********
changed: [test01.fale.io]

PLAY RECAP ***********************************************************
test01.fale.io      : ok=3    changed=2    unreachable=0    failed=0
```

Wow! The example worked. Let's now check whether the `httpd` package is installed and up-and-running on the machine. To check if HTTPd is installed, the easiest way is to ask `rpm`:

```
$ rpm -qa | grep httpd
```

If everything worked properly, you should have an output like the following:

```
httpd-tools-2.4.6-40.el7.centos.x86_64
httpd-2.4.6-40.el7.centos.x86_64
```

To see the status of the service, we can ask `systemd`:

```
$ systemctl status httpd
```

The expected result is something like the following:

```
httpd.service - The Apache HTTP Server
    Loaded: loaded (/usr/lib/systemd/system/httpd.service; enabled;
vendor preset: disabled)
    Active: active (running) since Sat 2016-05-07 13:22:14 EDT; 7min ago
      Docs: man:httpd(8)
            man:apachectl(8)
  Main PID: 2214 (httpd)
    Status: "Total requests: 0; Current requests/sec: 0; Current
traffic:   0 B/sec"
    CGroup: /system.slice/httpd.service
            -2214 /usr/sbin/httpd -DFOREGROUND
            -2215 /usr/sbin/httpd -DFOREGROUND
            -2216 /usr/sbin/httpd -DFOREGROUND
            -2217 /usr/sbin/httpd -DFOREGROUND
            -2218 /usr/sbin/httpd -DFOREGROUND
            -2219 /usr/sbin/httpd -DFOREGROUND
```

The end state, according to the playbook, has been achieved. Let's briefly look at exactly what happens during the playbook run:

```
PLAY [all] *************************************************************
```

This line advises us that a playbook is going to start here and that it will be executed on "`all`" hosts:

```
TASK [setup] ***********************************************************
ok: [test01.fale.io]
```

The `TASK` lines show the name of the task (`setup` in this case), and their effect on each host. Sometimes people get confused by the `setup` task. In fact, if you look at the playbook, there is no `setup` task. This is because Ansible, before executing the tasks that we have asked it to, will try to connect to the machine and gather information about it that could be useful later. As you can see, the task resulted with a green `ok` state, so it succeeded and nothing was changed on the server:

```
TASK [Ensure the HTTPd package is installed] ***********************
changed: [test01.fale.io]
TASK [Ensure the HTTPd service is enabled and running] ***********
changed: [test01.fale.io]
```

These two task's states are yellow and spell "`changed`". This means that those tasks were executed and have succeeded but have actually changed something on the machine:

```
PLAY RECAP *************************************************************
test01.fale.io          : ok=3    changed=2    unreachable=0    failed=0
```

Those last few lines are a recapitulation of how the playbook went. Let's rerun the task now and see the output after both the tasks have actually run:

```
PLAY [all] *************************************************************
TASK [setup] ***********************************************************
ok: [test01.fale.io]
TASK [Ensure the HTTPd package is installed] ***********************
ok: [test01.fale.io]
TASK [Ensure the HTTPd service is enabled and running] ***********
ok: [test01.fale.io]
PLAY RECAP *************************************************************
test01.fale.io          : ok=3    changed=0    unreachable=0    failed=0
```

As you would have expected, the two tasks in question give an output of `ok`, which would mean that the desired state was already met prior to running the task. It's important to remember that many tasks such as the **Gathering facts** task obtain information regarding a particular component of the system and do not necessarily change anything on the system; hence, these tasks didn't display the changed output earlier.

The `PLAY RECAP` section in the first and second run are shown as follows. You will see the following output during the first run:

```
PLAY RECAP *********************************************************
test01.fale.io         : ok=3    changed=2    unreachable=0    failed=0
```

You will see the following output during the second run:

```
PLAY RECAP *********************************************************
test01.fale.io         : ok=3    changed=0    unreachable=0    failed=0
```

As you can see, the difference is that the first task's output shows `changed=2`, which means that the system state changed twice due to two tasks. It's very useful to look at this output, since, if a system has achieved its desired state and then you run the playbook on it, the expected output should be `changed=0`.

If you're thinking of the word **Idempotency** at this stage, you're absolutely right and deserve a pat on the back! Idempotency is one of the key tenets of configuration management. Wikipedia defines Idempotency as an operation that, if applied twice to any value, gives the same result as if it were applied once. The earliest examples of this that you would have encountered in your childhood would be multiplicative operations on the number 1, where `1*1=1` every single time.

Most of the configuration management tools have taken this principle and applied it to the infrastructure as well. In a large infrastructure, it is highly recommended to monitor or track the number of changed tasks in your infrastructure and alert the concerned tasks if you find oddities; this applies to any configuration management tool in general. In an ideal state, the only time you should see changes is when you're introducing a new change in the form of any **Create**, **Remove**, **Update**, or **Delete** (**CRUD**) operation on various system components. If you're wondering how you can do it with Ansible, keep reading the book and you'll eventually find the answer!

## Automating Simple Tasks

Let's proceed. You could have also written the preceding tasks as follows but when the tasks are run, from an end user's perspective, they are quite readable (we will call this file `setup_apache_no_com.yaml`):

```yaml
---
- hosts: all
  remote_user: fale
  tasks:
  - yum:
      name: httpd
      state: present
    become: True
  - service:
      name: httpd
      state: started
      enabled: True
    become: True
```

Let's run the playbook again to spot any difference in the output:

```
$ ansible-playbook -i test01.fale.io, setup_apache_no_com.yaml
```

The output would be:

```
PLAY [all] *********************************************************
TASK [setup] *******************************************************
ok: [test01.fale.io]

TASK [yum] *********************************************************
ok: [test01.fale.io]

TASK [service] *****************************************************
ok: [test01.fale.io]

PLAY RECAP *********************************************************
test01.fale.io             : ok=3    changed=0    unreachable=0    failed=0
```

As you can see, the difference is in the readability. Wherever possible, it's recommended to keep the tasks as simple as possible (the **KISS** principle of **Keep It Simple Stupid**) to allow for maintainability of your scripts in the long run.

Now that we've seen how you can write a basic playbook and run it against a host, let's look at other options that would help you while running playbooks.

# Ansible verbosity

One of the first options anyone picks up is the debug option. To understand what is happening when you run the playbook, you can run it with the **verbose** (-v) option. Every extra v will provide the end user with more debug output.

Let's see an example of using the playbook debug for a single task using the following debug options:

- The -v option provides the default output, as shown in the preceding examples.
- The -vv option adds a little more information, as shown in the following example:

```
Using /etc/ansible/ansible.cfg as config file

PLAYBOOK: setup_apache.yaml ******************************
1 plays in setup_apache.yaml

PLAY [all] ***********************************************

TASK [setup] *********************************************
ok: [test01.fale.io]

TASK [Ensure the HTTPd package is installed] *************
task path: /home/fale/setup_apache.yaml:5
ok: [test01.fale.io] => {"changed": false, "msg": "", "rc": 0, "results": ["httpd-2.4.6-40.el7.centos.x86_64 providing httpd is already installed"]}

TASK [Ensure the HTTPd service is enabled and running] ****
task path: /home/fale/setup_apache.yaml:10
ok: [test01.fale.io] => {"changed": false, "enabled": true, "name": "httpd", "state": "started"}

PLAY RECAP ***********************************************
test01.fale.io    : ok=3    changed=0    unreachable=0    failed=0
```

- The -vvv option adds a lot more information, as shown in the following code. This shows the ssh command Ansible uses to create a temporary file on the remote host and run the script remotely:

```
TASK [Ensure the HTTPd package is installed] *************
task path: /home/fale/setup_apache.yaml:5
<test01.fale.io> ESTABLISH SSH CONNECTION FOR USER: fale
<test01.fale.io> SSH: EXEC ssh -C -q -o ControlMaster=auto -o ControlPersist=60s -o KbdInteractiveAuthentication=no -o
```

*Automating Simple Tasks*

```
PreferredAuthentications=gssapi-with-mic,gssapi-keyex,hostbased,publickey -
o PasswordAuthentication=no -o User=fale -o ConnectTimeout=10 -o
ControlPath=/home/fale/.ansible/cp/ansible-ssh-%C test01.fale.io '/bin/sh -
c '"'"'( umask 22 && mkdir -p "` echo $HOME/.ansible/tmp/ansible-
tmp-1462644055.19-51001413558638 `" && echo "` echo
$HOME/.ansible/tmp/ansible-tmp-1462644055.19-51001413558638 `" )'"'"''
        <test01.fale.io> PUT /tmp/tmp9JSYiP TO /home/fale/.ansible/tmp/ansible-
tmp-1462644055.19-51001413558638/yum
        <test01.fale.io> SSH: EXEC sftp -b - -C -o ControlMaster=auto -o
ControlPersist=60s -o KbdInteractiveAuthentication=no -o
PreferredAuthentications=gssapi-with-mic,gssapi-keyex,hostbased,publickey -
o PasswordAuthentication=no -o User=fale -o ConnectTimeout=10 -o
ControlPath=/home/fale/.ansible/cp/ansible-ssh-%C '[test01.fale.io]'
        <test01.fale.io> ESTABLISH SSH CONNECTION FOR USER: fale
        <test01.fale.io> SSH: EXEC ssh -C -q -o ControlMaster=auto -o
ControlPersist=60s -o KbdInteractiveAuthentication=no -o
PreferredAuthentications=gssapi-with-mic,gssapi-keyex,hostbased,publickey -
o PasswordAuthentication=no -o User=fale -o ConnectTimeout=10 -o
ControlPath=/home/fale/.ansible/cp/ansible-ssh-%C -tt test01.fale.io
'/bin/sh -c '"'"'sudo -H -S -n -u root /bin/sh -c '"'"'"'"'"'"'"'"'echo
BECOME-SUCCESS-axnwopicemeccmdhnlmhawtwlysgfgjc; LANG=en_US.utf8
LC_ALL=en_US.utf8 LC_MESSAGES=en_US.utf8 /usr/bin/python -tt
/home/fale/.ansible/tmp/ansible-tmp-1462644055.19-51001413558638/yum; rm -
rf "/home/fale/.ansible/tmp/ansible-tmp-1462644055.19-51001413558638/" >
/dev/null 2>&1'"'"'"'"'"'"'"'"''"'"''
        ok: [test01.fale.io] => {"changed": false, "invocation":
{"module_args": {"conf_file": null, "disable_gpg_check": false,
"disablerepo": null, "enablerepo": null, "exclude": null,
"install_repoquery": true, "list": null, "name": ["httpd"], "state":
"present", "update_cache": false}, "module_name": "yum"}, "msg": "", "rc":
0, "results": ["httpd-2.4.6-40.el7.centos.x86_64 providing httpd is already
installed"]}
```

# Variables in playbooks

Sometimes it is important to `set` and `get` variables in a playbook.

Very often, you'll need to automate multiple similar operations. In those cases, you'll want to create a single playbook that can be called with different variables to ensure code reusability.

Another case where variables are very important is when you have more than one datacenter and some values will be datacenter-specific. A common example are the DNS servers. Let's analyze the following simple code that will introduce us to the Ansible way to set and get variables:

```yaml
---
- hosts: all
  remote_user: fale
  tasks:
  - name: Set variable 'name'
    set_fact:
      name: Test machine
  - name: Print variable 'name'
    debug:
      msg: '{{ name }}'
```

Let's run it in the usual way:

```
$ ansible-playbook -i test01.fale.io, variables.yaml
```

You should see the following result:

```
PLAY [all] ************************************************************
TASK [setup] **********************************************************
ok: [test01.fale.io]

TASK [Set variable 'name'] ********************************************
ok: [test01.fale.io]

TASK [Print variable 'name'] ******************************************
ok: [test01.fale.io] => {
    "msg": "Test machine"
}

PLAY RECAP ************************************************************
test01.fale.io             : ok=3    changed=0    unreachable=0    failed=0
```

If we analyze the code we have just executed, it should be pretty clear what's going on. We set a variable (that in Ansible are called `facts`) and then we print it with the `debug` function.

Variables should always be between quotes when you use this expanded version of YAML.

*Automating Simple Tasks*

Ansible allows you to set your variables in many different ways, that is, either by passing a variable file, declaring it in a playbook, passing it to the `ansible-playbook` command using `-e` / `--extra-vars`, or by declaring it in an inventory file (we will be discussing more in-depth about this in the next chapter).

It's now time to start using some metadata that Ansible obtained during the setup phase. Let's start by looking at the data that is gathered by Ansible. To do this, we will execute:

```
$ ansible all -i HOST, -m setup
```

In our specific case, this means executing the following:

```
$ ansible all -i test01.fale.io, -m setup
```

We can obviously do the same with a playbook, but this way is faster. Also, for the "setup" case, you will need to see the output only during the development to be sure to use the right variable name for your goal.

The output will be something like this:

```
test01.fale.io | SUCCESS => {
    "ansible_facts": {
        "ansible_all_ipv4_addresses": [
            "178.62.36.208",
            "10.16.0.7"
        ],
        "ansible_all_ipv6_addresses": [
            "fe80::601:e2ff:fef1:1301"
        ],
        "ansible_architecture": "x86_64",
        "ansible_bios_date": "04/25/2016",
        "ansible_bios_version": "20160425",
        "ansible_cmdline": {
            "ro": true,
            "root": "LABEL=DOROOT"
        },
        "ansible_date_time": {
            "date": "2016-05-14",
            "day": "14",
            "epoch": "1463244633",
            "hour": "12",
            "iso8601": "2016-05-14T16:50:33Z",
            "iso8601_basic": "20160514T125033231663",
            "iso8601_basic_short": "20160514T125033",
            "iso8601_micro": "2016-05-14T16:50:33.231770Z",
            "minute": "50",
            "month": "05",
```

```
            "second": "33",
            "time": "12:50:33",
            "tz": "EDT",
            "tz_offset": "-0400",
            "weekday": "Saturday",
            "weekday_number": "6",
            "weeknumber": "19",
            "year": "2016"
        },
        "ansible_default_ipv4": {
            "address": "178.62.36.208",
            "alias": "eth0",
            "broadcast": "178.62.63.255",
            "gateway": "178.62.0.1",
            "interface": "eth0",
            "macaddress": "04:01:e2:f1:13:01",
            "mtu": 1500,
            "netmask": "255.255.192.0",
            "network": "178.62.0.0",
            "type": "ether"
        },
        "ansible_default_ipv6": {},
        "ansible_devices": {
            "vda": {
                "holders": [],
                "host": "",
                "model": null,
                "partitions": {
                    "vda1": {
                        "sectors": "41943040",
                        "sectorsize": 512,
                        "size": "20.00 GB",
                        "start": "2048"
                    }
                },
                "removable": "0",
                "rotational": "1",
                "scheduler_mode": "",
                "sectors": "41947136",
                "sectorsize": "512",
                "size": "20.00 GB",
                "support_discard": "0",
                "vendor": "0x1af4"
            }
        },
        "ansible_distribution": "CentOS",
        "ansible_distribution_major_version": "7",
        "ansible_distribution_release": "Core",
```

```
            "ansible_distribution_version": "7.2.1511",
        "ansible_dns": {
            "nameservers": [
                "8.8.8.8",
                "8.8.4.4"
            ]
        },
        "ansible_domain": "",
        "ansible_env": {
            "HOME": "/home/fale",
            "LANG": "en_US.utf8",
            "LC_ALL": "en_US.utf8",
            "LC_MESSAGES": "en_US.utf8",
            "LESSOPEN": "||/usr/bin/lesspipe.sh %s",
            "LOGNAME": "fale",
            "MAIL": "/var/mail/fale",
            "PATH": "/usr/local/bin:/usr/bin",
            "PWD": "/home/fale",
            "SHELL": "/bin/bash",
            "SHLVL": "2",
            "SSH_CLIENT": "86.187.141.39 37764 22",
            "SSH_CONNECTION": "86.187.141.39 37764 178.62.36.208 22",
            "SSH_TTY": "/dev/pts/0",
            "TERM": "rxvt-unicode-256color",
            "USER": "fale",
            "XDG_RUNTIME_DIR": "/run/user/1000",
            "XDG_SESSION_ID": "180",
            "_": "/usr/bin/python"
        },
        "ansible_eth0": {
            "active": true,
            "device": "eth0",
            "ipv4": {
                "address": "178.62.36.208",
                "broadcast": "178.62.63.255",
                "netmask": "255.255.192.0",
                "network": "178.62.0.0"
            },
            "ipv4_secondaries": [
                {
                    "address": "10.16.0.7",
                    "broadcast": "10.16.255.255",
                    "netmask": "255.255.0.0",
                    "network": "10.16.0.0"
                }
            ],
            "ipv6": [
                {
```

```
                    "address": "fe80::601:e2ff:fef1:1301",
                    "prefix": "64",
                    "scope": "link"
                }
            ],
            "macaddress": "04:01:e2:f1:13:01",
            "module": "virtio_net",
            "mtu": 1500,
            "pciid": "virtio0",
            "promisc": false,
            "type": "ether"
        },
        "ansible_eth1": {
            "active": false,
            "device": "eth1",
            "macaddress": "04:01:e2:f1:13:02",
            "module": "virtio_net",
            "mtu": 1500,
            "pciid": "virtio1",
            "promisc": false,
            "type": "ether"
        },
        "ansible_fips": false,
        "ansible_form_factor": "Other",
        "ansible_fqdn": "test",
        "ansible_hostname": "test",
        "ansible_interfaces": [
            "lo",
            "eth1",
            "eth0"
        ],
        "ansible_kernel": "3.10.0-327.10.1.el7.x86_64",
        "ansible_lo": {
            "active": true,
            "device": "lo",
            "ipv4": {
                "address": "127.0.0.1",
                "broadcast": "host",
                "netmask": "255.0.0.0",
                "network": "127.0.0.0"
            },
            "ipv6": [
                {
                    "address": "::1",
                    "prefix": "128",
                    "scope": "host"
                }
            ],
```

```
            "mtu": 65536,
            "promisc": false,
            "type": "loopback"
    },
    "ansible_machine": "x86_64",
    "ansible_machine_id": "fd8cf26e06e411e4a9d004010897bd01",
    "ansible_memfree_mb": 6,
    "ansible_memory_mb": {
        "nocache": {
            "free": 381,
            "used": 108
        },
        "real": {
            "free": 6,
            "total": 489,
            "used": 483
        },
        "swap": {
            "cached": 0,
            "free": 0,
            "total": 0,
            "used": 0
        }
    },
    "ansible_memtotal_mb": 489,
    "ansible_mounts": [
        {
            "device": "/dev/vda1",
            "fstype": "ext4",
            "mount": "/",
            "options": "rw,relatime,data=ordered",
            "size_available": 18368385024,
            "size_total": 21004894208,
            "uuid": "c5845b43-fe98-499a-bf31-4eccae14261b"
        }
    ],
    "ansible_nodename": "test",
    "ansible_os_family": "RedHat",
    "ansible_pkg_mgr": "yum",
    "ansible_processor": [
        "GenuineIntel",
        "Intel(R) Xeon(R) CPU E5-2630L v2 @ 2.40GHz"
    ],
    "ansible_processor_cores": 1,
    "ansible_processor_count": 1,
    "ansible_processor_threads_per_core": 1,
    "ansible_processor_vcpus": 1,
    "ansible_product_name": "Droplet",
```

```
            "ansible_product_serial": "NA",
            "ansible_product_uuid": "NA",
            "ansible_product_version": "20160415",
            "ansible_python_version": "2.7.5",
            "ansible_selinux": {
                "status": "disabled"
            },
            "ansible_service_mgr": "systemd",
            "ansible_ssh_host_key_dsa_public":
"AAAAB3NzaC1kc3MAAACBAPEf4dzeET6ukHemTASsamoRLxo2R8iHg5J1bYQUyuggtRK1bRrHMt
pQ8qN5CQNtp8J+2Hq6/JKiDF+cdxgOehf9b7F4araVvJxqx967RvLNBrMWXv7/4hi+efgXG9eej
GoGQNAD66up/fkLMd0L8fwSwmTJoZXwOxFwcbnxCZsFAAAAFQDgK7fka+1AKjYZNFIfCB2b0Zit
GQAAAIADeofiC5q+SLgEvkBCUCTyJ+EVb6WHeHbVdrpE2GdnUr03R6MmmYhYZMijruS/rcpzBLm
i8juDkqAWy6Xqxd+DwixykntXPeUFS3F7LK5vNwFaIaRltPwr4Azh+EeSUQ2Zz2AdKx6zSqtLOD
8ZMPkRDvz4WGHGmeR+i7UFsFDZdgAAAIEAy26Tx0jAlY3mEaTW91Q9DoGXgPBxsSX/XqeLh5wBa
BO6AJaIrs0dQJdNeHcMhFy0seVkOMN1SpeoBTJSoTOx15HAGsKsAcmnA5mcJeUZqptVR6JxROzt
Hw3zQePQ3/V3KQzAN31tIm3PbKzt1EZbXRUM7RV5WsdRHTb8rutENhY=",
            "ansible_ssh_host_key_ecdsa_public":
"AAAAE2VjZHNhLXNoYTItbmlzdHAyNTYAAAAIbmlzdHAyNTYAAABBBPDXQ9rjgDmUKsEWH4U2vg
4iqtK+75urlj9nwW+rNNTFHTE5oG82sOlO6o0tUY8LXgB/tJnIcJ1hINdrWrZNpn4=",
            "ansible_ssh_host_key_rsa_public":
"AAAAB3NzaC1yc2EAAAADAQABAAABAQCwQx5EElH7FeD/agB/gCJfBUEVhk44tldzdEzwc2IEbI
59relTGNOU7soCCMcSH7nwlEbOOvmLa2R/YaXdHv/cb1aXBC/wj/m4ZHylBeF5qzECUkeaB3+CT
+hp8qHHApclFr21m2CwZ+YXjEyjJ3en4K3gLlIQyQjgE2F57kmD1FVVDSJFvNTn+NQvb3DPppND
+HKEeHwrJ0GgznoP62yobEgriAIBSGf//OWHCO/9shEvauoRpPM+U9pU7lv637s7qyubIqyrs5f
z3u34qBj8oCATOefRN1wsfJDeMG0D5ryI6BI6t/eAi8BPr7VHJSQBk+buM9Jr1yoMQTEasq2J",
            "ansible_swapfree_mb": 0,
            "ansible_swaptotal_mb": 0,
            "ansible_system": "Linux",
            "ansible_system_vendor": "DigitalOcean",
            "ansible_uptime_seconds": 603067,
            "ansible_user_dir": "/home/fale",
            "ansible_user_gecos": "",
            "ansible_user_gid": 1000,
            "ansible_user_id": "fale",
            "ansible_user_shell": "/bin/bash",
            "ansible_user_uid": 1000,
            "ansible_userspace_architecture": "x86_64",
            "ansible_userspace_bits": "64",
            "ansible_virtualization_role": "host",
            "ansible_virtualization_type": "kvm",
            "module_setup": true
        },
        "changed": false
    }
```

*Automating Simple Tasks*

As you can see, from this huge list of options, you can gain a huge quantity of information, and you can use them as any other variable. Let's print the OS name and the version. To do so, we can create a new playbook called `setup_variables.yaml` with the following content:

```yaml
---
- hosts: all
  remote_user: fale
  tasks:
  - name: Print OS and version
    debug:
      msg: '{{ ansible_distribution }} {{ ansible_distribution_version }}'
```

Run it with the following:

```
$ ansible-playbook -itest01.fale.io, setup_variables.yaml
```

This will give us the following output:

```
PLAY [all] *********************************************************
TASK [setup] *******************************************************
ok: [test01.fale.io]

TASK [Print OS and version] ****************************************
ok: [test01.fale.io] => {
    "msg": "CentOS 7.2.1511"
}

PLAY RECAP *********************************************************
test01.fale.io      : ok=2    changed=0    unreachable=0    failed=0
```

As you can see, it printed the OS name and version, as expected. In addition to the methods seen previously, it's also possible to pass a variable using a command-line argument. In fact, if we look in the Ansible help, we will notice the following:

```
-e EXTRA_VARS, --extra-vars=EXTRA_VARS
set additional variables as key=value or YAML/JSON
```

The same lines are present in the `ansible-playbook` command as well. Let's make a small playbook called `cli_variables.yaml` with the following content:

```yaml
---
- hosts: all
  remote_user: fale
  tasks:
  - name: Print variable 'name'
    debug:
      msg: '{{ name }}'
```

Execute it with the following:

```
$ ansible-playbook -i test01.fale.io, cli_variables.yaml -e 'name=test01'
```

We will receive the following:

```
PLAY [all] ********************************************************
TASK [setup] ******************************************************
ok: [test01.fale.io]
TASK [Print variable 'name'] **************************************
ok: [test01.fale.io] => {
    "msg": "test01"
}
PLAY RECAP ********************************************************
test01.fale.io     : ok=2    changed=0    unreachable=0    failed=0
```

In case we forgot to add the additional parameter to specify the variable, we would have executed it as:

```
$ ansible-playbook -i test01.fale.io, cli_variables.yaml
```

We would have received the following output:

```
PLAY [all] ********************************************************
TASK [setup] ******************************************************
ok: [test01.fale.io]

TASK [Print variable 'name'] **************************************
    fatal: [test01.fale.io]: FAILED! => {"failed": true, "msg": "'name' is undefined"}

NO MORE HOSTS LEFT ************************************************
to retry, use: --limit @cli_variables.retry

PLAY RECAP ********************************************************
test01.fale.io     : ok=1    changed=0    unreachable=0    failed=1
```

Now that we have learned the basics of playbooks, let's create a web server from scratch using them. To do so, let's start from the beginning, creating an Ansible user and then moving forward from there.

## Creating the Ansible user

When you create a machine (or rent one from any hosting company) it arrives only with the `root` user. Let's start creating a playbook that ensures that an Ansible user is created, it's accessible with an SSH key, and is able to perform actions on behalf of other users (`sudo`) with no password asked. I often call this playbook, `firstrun.yaml` since I execute it as soon as a new machine is created, but after that, I don't use it since it uses the root user that I disable for security reasons. Our script will look something like the following:

```yaml
---
- hosts: all
  user: root
  tasks:
  - name: Ensure ansible user exists
    user:
      name: ansible
      state: present
      comment: Ansible
  - name: Ensure ansible user accepts the SSH key
    authorized_key:
      user: ansible
      key: https://github.com/fale.keys
    state: present
  - name: Ensure the ansible user is sudoer with no password required
    lineinfile:
      dest: /etc/sudoers
      state: present
      regexp: '^ansible ALL\='
      line: 'ansible ALL=(ALL) NOPASSWD:ALL'
      validate: 'visudo -cf %s'
```

Before running it, let's look at it a little bit. We have used three different modules (`user`, `authorized_key`, and `lineinfile`) that we have never seen. The `user` module, as the name suggests, allows us to make sure a user is present (or absent).

The `authorized_key` module allows us to ensure that a certain SSH key can be used to login as a specific user on that machine. This module will not substitute all the SSH keys that are already enabled for that user, but will simply add (or remove) the specified key. If you want to alter this behavior, you can use the *exclusive* option, that allows you to delete all the SSH keys that are not specified in this step.

The `lineinfile` module allows us to alter the content of a file. It works in a very similar way to **sed** (a stream editor), where you specify the regular expression that will be used to match the line, and then specify the new line that will be used to substitute the matched line. If no line is matched, the line is added at the end of the file. Now let's run it with:

```
$ ansible-playbook -i test01.fale.io, firstrun.yaml
```

This will give us the following result:

```
PLAY [all] ***********************************************
TASK [setup] *********************************************
ok: [test01.fale.io]

TASK [Ensure ansible user exists] ********************************
changed: [test01.fale.io]

TASK [Ensure ansible user accepts the SSH key] ******************
changed: [test01.fale.io]

TASK [Ensure the anisble user is sudoer with no password required] *
changed: [test01.fale.io]

PLAY RECAP ***********************************************
test01.fale.io       : ok=4    changed=3    unreachable=0    failed=0
```

## Configuring a basic server

After we have created the user for Ansible with the necessary privileges, we can go on to make some other small changes to the OS. To make it more clear, we will see how each action is performed and then we'll look at the whole playbook.

### Enabling EPEL

EPEL is the most important repository for Enterprise Linux and it contains a lot of additional packages. It's also a safe repository since no package in EPEL will conflict with packages in the base repository. To enable EPEL in RHEL/CentOS 7, it is enough to just install the `epel-release` package. To do so in Ansible, we will use:

```
- name: Ensure EPEL is enabled
  yum:
    name: epel-release
    state: present
  become: True
```

*Automating Simple Tasks*

As you can see, we have used the `yum` module, as we did in one of the first examples of the chapter, specifying the name of the package and that we want it to be present.

## Installing Python bindings for SELinux

Since Ansible is written in Python and mainly uses the Python bindings to operate on the operating system, we will need to install the Python bindings for SELinux:

```
- name: Ensure libselinux-python is present
  yum:
    name: libselinux-python
    state: present
  become: True
- name: Ensure libsemanage-python is present
  yum:
    name: libsemanage-python
    state: present
  become: True
```

This could be written in a shorter way, using a cycle, but we'll see how to do so in the next chapter.

## Upgrading all installed packages

To upgrade all installed packages, we will need to use the `yum` module again, but with a different parameter, in fact we would use:

```
- name: Ensure we have last version of every package
  yum:
    name: "*"
    state: latest
  become: True
```

As you can see, we have specified "*" as the package name (this stands for a wildcard to match all installed packages) and the `state` is `latest`. This will upgrade all installed packages to the latest version available.

If you remember, when we talked about the "`present`" state, we said that it was going to install the last available version. So what's the difference between "`present`" and "`latest`"? Present will install the latest version if the package is not installed, while if the package is already installed (no matter the version) it will go forward without making any change. Latest will install the latest version if the package is not installed, while if the package is already installed will check whether a newer version is available and if it is, Ansible will update the package.

## Ensuring that NTP is installed, configured, and running

To make sure NTP is present, we use the `yum` module:

```
- name: Ensure NTP is installed
  yum:
    name: ntp
    state: present
  become: True
```

Now that we know that NTP is installed, we should ensure that the server is using the `timezone` that we want. To do so, we will create a symbolic link in `/etc/localtime` that will point to the wanted `zoneinfo` file:

```
- name: Ensure the timezone is set to UTC
  file:
    src: /usr/share/zoneinfo/GMT
    dest: /etc/localtime
    state: link
  become: True
```

As you can see, we have used the `file` module to tell Ansible, specifying that it needs to be a link (`state: link`).

To complete the NTP configuration, we need to start the `ntpd` service and ensure that it will run at every, consequent boot:

```
- name: Ensure the NTP service is running and enabled
  service:
    name: ntpd
    state: started
    enabled: True
  become: True
```

# Ensuring that FirewallD is present and enabled

As you can imagine, the first step is to ensure that FirewallD is installed:

```
- name: Ensure FirewallD is installed
  yum:
    name: firewalld
    state: present
  become: True
```

Since we want to be sure that, when we enable FirewallD we will not lose our SSH connection, we ensure that SSH traffic can always pass through it:

```
- name: Ensure SSH can pass the firewall
  firewalld:
    service: ssh
    state: enabled
    permanent: True
    immediate: True
  become: True
```

To do so, we have used the `firewalld` module. This module will take parameters that are very similar to the ones the `firewall-cmd` console would use. You will have to specify the service that is to be authorized to pass the firewall, whether you want this rule to apply immediately, and whether you want the rule to be permanent so that after a reboot the rule will still be present.

> You can specify the service name (such as `'ssh'`) using the `service` parameter, or you can specify the port (such as `'22/tcp'`) using the `port` parameter.

Now that we have installed FirewallD and we are sure that our SSH connection will survive, we can enable it as we do any other service:

```
- name: Ensure FirewallD is running
  service:
    name: firewalld
    state: started
    enabled: True
  become: True
```

# Adding a customized MOTD

To add the MOTD, we will need a template that will be the same for all servers and a task to use the template.

I find it very useful to add a MOTD to every server. It's even more useful if you use Ansible, because you can use it to warn your users that changes to the system could be overwritten by Ansible. My usual template is called 'motd', and has this content:

```
            This system is managed by Ansible
    Any change done on this system could be overwritten by Ansible
OS: {{ ansible_distribution }} {{ ansible_distribution_version }}
Hostname: {{ inventory_hostname }}
eth0 address: {{ ansible_eth0.ipv4.address }}
All connections are monitored and recorded
    Disconnect IMMEDIATELY if you are not an authorized user
```

This is a `jinja2` template and it allows us to use every variable set in the playbooks. This also allows us to use complex syntax for conditionals and cycles that we will see later in this chapter. To populate a file from a template in Ansible, we will need to use:

```
- name: Ensure the MOTD file is present and updated
  template:
    src: motd
    dest: /etc/motd
    owner: root
    group: root
    mode: 0644
  become: True
```

The template module allows us to specify a local file (`src`) that will be interpreted by `jinja2` and the output of this operation will be saved on the remote machine in a specific path (`dest`), be owned by a specific user (`owner`) and group (`group`), and have a specific access mode (`mode`).

# Changing the hostname

To keep things simple, one way I find useful is to set the hostname of a machine to something meaningful. To do so, we can use a very simple Ansible module called `hostname`:

```
- name: Ensure the hostname is the same of the inventory
  hostname:
    name: "{{ inventory_hostname }}"
  become: True
```

# Reviewing and running the playbook

Putting everything together, we now have the following playbook (called `common_tasks.yaml` for simplicity):

```
---
- hosts: all
  remote_user: ansible
  tasks:
  - name: Ensure EPEL is enabled
    yum:
      name: epel-release
      state: present
    become: True
  - name: Ensure libselinux-python is present
    yum:
      name: libselinux-python
      state: present
    become: True
  - name: Ensure libsemanage-python is present
    yum:
      name: libsemanage-python
      state: present
    become: True
  - name: Ensure we have last version of every package
    yum:
      name: "*"
      state: latest
    become: True
  - name: Ensure NTP is installed
    yum:
      name: ntp
      state: present
    become: True
  - name: Ensure the timezone is set to UTC
```

```yaml
    file:
      src: /usr/share/zoneinfo/GMT
      dest: /etc/localtime
      state: link
    become: True
  - name: Ensure the NTP service is running and enabled
    service:
      name: ntpd
      state: started
      enabled: True
    become: True
  - name: Ensure FirewallD is installed
    yum:
      name: firewalld
      state: present
    become: True
  - name: Ensure FirewallD is running
    service:
      name: firewalld
      state: started
      enabled: True
    become: True
  - name: Ensure SSH can pass the firewall
    firewalld:
      service: ssh
      state: enabled
      permanent: True
      immediate: True
    become: True
  - name: Ensure the MOTD file is present and updated
    template:
      src: motd
      dest: /etc/motd
      owner: root
      group: root
      mode: 0644
    become: True
  - name: Ensure the hostname is the same of the inventory
    hostname:
      name: "{{ inventory_hostname }}"
    become: True
```

*Automating Simple Tasks*

Since this `playbook` is pretty complex, we can run the following:

```
$ ansible-playbook common_tasks.yaml --list-tasks
```

This asks Ansible to print all the tasks in a shorter form so that we can quickly see what tasks a `playbook` performs. The output should be something like the following:

```
playbook: common_tasks.yaml
  play #1 (all): all TAGS: []
    tasks:
      Ensure EPEL is enabled TAGS: []
      Ensure libselinux-python is present TAGS: []
      Ensure libsemanage-python is present TAGS: []
      Ensure we have last version of every package TAGS: []
      Ensure NTP is installed TAGS: []
      Ensure the timezone is set to UTC TAGS: []
      Ensure the NTP service is running and enabled TAGS: []
      Ensure FirewallD is installed TAGS: []
      Ensure FirewallD is running TAGS: []
      Ensure SSH can pass the firewall TAGS: []
      Ensure the MOTD file is present and updated TAGS: []
      Ensure the hostname is the same of the inventory TAGS: []
```

We can now run the `playbook` with the following:

```
$ ansible-playbook -itest01.fale.io, common_tasks.yaml
```

We will receive the following output:

```
PLAY [all] *********************************************************

TASK [setup] *******************************************************
ok: [test01.fale.io]

TASK [Ensure EPEL is enabled] **************************************
changed: [test01.fale.io]

TASK [Ensure libselinux-python is present] *************************
ok: [test01.fale.io]

TASK [Esure libsemanage-python is present] *************************
ok: [test01.fale.io]

TASK [Ensure we have last version of every package] ****************
changed: [test01.fale.io]

TASK [Ensure NTP is installed] *************************************
ok: [test01.fale.io]
```

```
TASK [Ensure the timezone is set to UTC] *************************
changed: [test01.fale.io]

TASK [Ensure the NTP service is running and enabled] ************
changed: [test01.fale.io]

TASK [Ensure FirewallD is installed] *****************************
ok: [test01.fale.io]
TASK [Ensure FirewallD is running] *******************************
changed: [test01.fale.io]

TASK [Ensure SSH can pass the firewall] **************************
ok: [test01.fale.io]

TASK [Ensure the MOTD file is present and updated] **************
changed: [test01.fale.io]

TASK [Ensure the hostname is the same of the inventory] **********
changed: [test01.fale.io]

PLAY RECAP *******************************************************
test01.fale.io         : ok=9    changed=7    unreachable=0    failed=0
```

# Installing and configuring a web server

Now that we have made some generic changes to the operating system, let's move on to actually creating a web server. We are splitting those two phases so we can share the first phase between every machine and apply the second only to web servers.

For this second phase, we will create a new playbook called `webserver.yaml` with the following content:

```
---
- hosts: all
  remote_user: ansible
  tasks:
  - name: Ensure the HTTPd package is installed
    yum:
      name: httpd
      state: present
    become: True
  - name: Ensure the HTTPd service is enabled and running
    service:
      name: httpd
      state: started
      enabled: True
```

```
      become: True
    - name: Ensure HTTP can pass the firewall
      firewalld:
        service: http
        state: enabled
        permanent: True
        immediate: True
      become: True
    - name: Ensure HTTPS can pass the firewall
      firewalld:
        service: https
        state: enabled
        permanent: True
        immediate: True
      become: True
```

As you can see, the first two tasks are the same as the ones in the example at the beginning of this chapter, and the last two tasks are used to instruct FirewallD to let HTTP and HTTPS traffic pass.

Let's run this script with the following:

```
$ ansible-playbook -i test01.fale.io, webserver.yaml
```

This results in the following:

```
PLAY [all] **********************************************************
TASK [setup] ********************************************************
ok: [test01.fale.io]

TASK [Ensure the HTTPd package is installed] ********************
changed: [test01.fale.io]

TASK [Ensure the HTTPd service is enabled and running] **********
changed: [test01.fale.io]

TASK [Ensure HTTP can pass the firewall] ************************
changed: [test01.fale.io]

TASK [Ensure HTTPS can pass the firewall] ***********************
changed: [test01.fale.io]

PLAY RECAP **********************************************************
test01.fale.io     : ok=5    changed=4    unreachable=0    failed=0
```

Now that we have a web server, let's publish a small single-page static website.

## Publishing a website

Since our website will be a simple, single page website, we can easily create it and publish it using a single Ansible task. To make this page a little bit more interesting, we will create it from a template that will be populated by Ansible with a little data about the machine. The script to publish it will be called `deploy_website.yaml` and will have the following content:

```yaml
---
- hosts: all
  remote_user: ansible
  tasks:
  - name: Ensure the website is present and updated
    template:
      src: index.html.j2
      dest: /var/www/html/index.html
      owner: root
      group: root
      mode: 0644
    become: True
```

Let's start with a simple template that we will call `index.html.j2`:

```
<html>
    <body>
        <h1>Hello World!</h1>
    </body>
</html>
```

Now we can test our website deployment by running the following:

```
$ ansible-playbook -i test01.fale.io, deploy_website.yaml
```

We should receive the following output:

```
PLAY [all] *********************************************************
TASK [setup] *******************************************************
ok: [test01.fale.io]

TASK [Ensure the website is present and updated] *******************
changed: [test01.fale.io]

PLAY RECAP *********************************************************
test01.fale.io      : ok=2    changed=1    unreachable=0    failed=0
```

If you now go to your test machine IP/FQDN in your browser, you'll find the "Hello World!" page.

# Jinja2 templates

**Jinja2** is a widely-used and fully-featured template engine for Python. Let's look at some syntax that will help us with Ansible. This paragraph does not want to be a replacement for the official documentation, but its goal is to teach you some components that you'll find very useful when using them with Ansible.

## Variables

As we have seen, we can print variable content simply with the `'{{ VARIABLE_NAME }}'` syntax. If we want to print just an element of an array we can use `'{{ ARRAY_NAME['KEY'] }}'`, and if we want to print a property of an object, we can use `'{{ OBJECT_NAME.PROPERTY_NAME }}'`.

So we can improve our previous static page in the following way:

```
<html>
    <body>
        <h1>Hello World!</h1>
        <p>This page was created on {{ ansible_date_time.date }}.</p>
    </body>
</html>
```

## Filters

From time to time, we may want to change the style of a string a little bit, without writing specific code for it, for example, we may want to capitalize some text. To do so, we can use one of Jinja2's filters, such as: `'{{ VARIABLE_NAME | capitalize }}'`. There are many filters available for Jinja2 and you can find the full list at: http://jinja.pocoo.org/docs/dev/templates/#builtin-filters.

## Conditionals

One thing you may often find useful in a template engine is the possibility of printing different strings depending on the content (or existence) of a string. So we can improve our static web page in the following way:

```
<html>
    <body>
        <h1>Hello World!</h1>
```

```
        <p>This page was created on {{ ansible_date_time.date }}.</p>
{% if ansible_eth0.active == True %}
        <p>eth0 address {{ ansible_eth0.ipv4.address }}.</p>
{% endif %}
    </body>
</html>
```

As you can see, we have added the capability to print the main IPv4 address for the eth0 connection, if the connection is active. With conditionals we can also use the tests.

 For a full list, please refer to: http://jinja.pocoo.org/docs/dev/templates/#builtin-tests.

So to obtain the same result we could also have written the following:

```
<html>
    <body>
        <h1>Hello World!</h1>
        <p>This page was created on {{ ansible_date_time.date }}.</p>
{% if ansible_eth0.active is equalto True %}
        <p>eth0 address {{ ansible_eth0.ipv4.address }}.</p>
{% endif %}
    </body>
</html>
```

There are a lot of different tests that will really help you to create easy-to-read, effective templates.

# Cycles

The jinja2 template system also offers the capability to create cycles. Let's add a feature to our page that will print the main IPv4 network address for each device instead of only eth0. We will then have the following code:

```
<html>
    <body>
        <h1>Hello World!</h1>
        <p>This page was created on {{ ansible_date_time.date }}.</p>
        <p>This machine can be reached on the following IP addresses</p>
        <ul>
{% for address in ansible_all_ipv4_addresses %}
            <li>{{ address }}</li>
{% endfor %}
```

```
            </ul>
        </body>
</html>
```

As you can see, the syntax for cycles is familiar if you already know Python.

These few pages on Jinja2 templating were not a substitute for the official documentation. In fact Jinja2 templates are much more powerful than what we have seen here. The goal here is only to give you the basic Jinja2 templates that are most often used in Ansible.

# Summary

In this chapter, we started looking at YAML and saw what a playbook is, how it works, and how to use it to create a web server (and a deployment for your static website). We have also seen multiple Ansible modules such as the user, yum, service, FirewalID, lineinfile, and template modules. At the end of the chapter, we focused on templates.

In the next chapter, we will talk about inventories so that we can easily manage multiple machines.

# 3
# Scaling to Multiple Hosts

In the previous chapters, we have specified the hosts in the command line. This worked fine while having a single host to work on, but will not work very well when managing multiple servers. In this chapter, we will see exactly how to manage multiple servers.

We'll explore the following topics:

- Ansible inventories
- Ansible host/group variables
- Ansible loops

## Working with inventory files

An inventory file is the source of truth for Ansible (there is also an advanced concept called **dynamic inventory**, which we will cover later). It follows the **Initialization** (**INI**) format and tells Ansible whether the remote host or hosts provided by the user are genuine.

Ansible can run its tasks against multiple hosts in parallel. To do this, you can directly pass the list of hosts to Ansible using an inventory file. For such parallel execution, Ansible allows you to group your hosts in the inventory file; the file passes the group name to Ansible. Ansible will search for that group in the inventory file and run its tasks against all the hosts listed in that group.

You can pass the inventory file to Ansible using the `-i` or `--inventory-file` option followed by the path to the file. If you do not explicitly specify any inventory file to Ansible, it will take the default path from the `host_file` parameter of `ansible.cfg`, which defaults to `/etc/ansible/hosts`.

*Scaling to Multiple Hosts*

When using the -i parameter, if the value is a list (it contains at least one comma) it will be used as the inventory list, while if the variable is a string, it will be used as the inventory file path.

## The basic inventory file

Before diving into the concept, let's first look at a basic inventory file called **hosts** that we can use instead of the list we used in the previous examples:

```
test01.fale.io
```

Ansible can take either a FQDN or an IP address within the inventory file.

We can now perform the same operations that we did in the previous chapter, tweaking the Ansible command parameters. For instance, to install the web server, we used this command:

```
$ ansible-playbook -i test01.fale.io, webserver.yaml
```

Instead, we can use the following:

```
$ ansible-playbook -i hosts webserver.yaml
```

As you can see, we have substituted the list of hosts with the inventory file name.

## Groups in an inventory file

The advantages of inventory files are noticeable when we have more complex situations. Let's say our website is getting more complicated and we now need a more complex environment. In our example, our website will require a MySQL database. Also we decide to have two web servers. In this scenario it makes sense to group different machines based on their role in our infrastructure. Our hosts file would change to:

```
[webserver]
ws01.fale.io
ws02.fale.io

[database]
db01.fale.io
```

Now we can instruct playbooks to run only on hosts in a certain group. We have created three different playbooks for our website example:

- `firstrun.yaml` is generic and will have to be run on every machine
- `common_tasks.yaml` is generic and will have to be run on every machine
- `webserver.yaml` is specific for web servers and therefore should not be run on any other machines

We need to change only the `webserver.yaml` file which, at the moment, specifies that it has to be run on all machines and should become web server only. To do so, let's open the `webserver.yaml` file and change content from:

```
- hosts: all
```

to:

```
- hosts: webserver
```

With only those three playbooks, we cannot proceed to create our environment with three servers. Since we don't have a playbook to set up the database yet (we will see it in the next chapter), we will provision the two web servers completely and for the database server we will only provision the base system.

We can run the `firstrun` playbook with the following:

```
$ ansible-playbook -i hosts firstrun.yaml
```

The following would be the result:

```
PLAY [all] ********************************************************
TASK [setup] ******************************************************
ok: [ws02.fale.io]
ok: [db01.fale.io]
ok: [ws01.fale.io]

TASK [Ensure ansible user exists] *********************************
changed: [ws01.fale.io]
changed: [db01.fale.io]
changed: [ws02.fale.io]

TASK [Ensure ansible user accepts the SSH key] ********************
changed: [ws02.fale.io]
changed: [ws01.fale.io]
changed: [db01.fale.io]

TASK [Ensure the ansible user is sudoer with no password required]
```

*Scaling to Multiple Hosts*

```
changed: [ws01.fale.io]
changed: [db01.fale.io]
changed: [ws02.fale.io]

PLAY RECAP ********************************************************
db01.fale.io              : ok=4      changed=3      unreachable=0      failed=0
ws01.fale.io              : ok=4      changed=3      unreachable=0      failed=0
ws02.fale.io              : ok=4      changed=3      unreachable=0      failed=0
```

As you can see, the output is very similar to what we received with a single host, but with one line per host at each step. In this case, all the machines were in the same state and the same steps have been performed, so we see that they all acted the same, but with more complex scenarios, you can have different machines returning different states on the same step. We can also execute the other two playbooks with similar results.

## Regular expressions in the inventory file

When you have a large number of servers, it is common and helpful to give them predictable names, for instance, call all web servers `wsXY` or `webXY`, or call the database servers `dbXY`. If you do so, you can reduce the number of lines in your `hosts` file increasing its readability. For instance, our `hosts` file can be simplified as:

```
[webserver]
ws[01:02].fale.io

[database]
db01.fale.io
```

In this example, we have used `[01:02]` that will match for all occurrences between the first number (`01` in our case) and the last (`02` in our case). In our case, the gain is not huge, but if you have 40 web servers, you can cut 39 lines from your `hosts` file.

## Working with variables

Ansible allows you to define variables in many ways, from a variable file within a playbook, by passing it from the Ansible command using the `-e` / `--extra-vars` option, or by passing it to an inventory file. You can define variables in an inventory file either on a per-host basis, for an entire group, or by creating a variable file in the directory where your inventory file exists.

## Host variables

It's possible to declare variables for a specific host, declaring them in the `hosts` file. For instance, we may want to specify different engines for our web servers. Let's suppose that one needs to reply to a specific domain, while the other to a different domain name. In this case, we would do it with the following `hosts` file:

```
[webserver]
ws01.fale.io domainname=example1.fale.io
ws02.fale.io domainname=example2.fale.io

[database]
db01.fale.io
```

In this way, all playbooks running on web servers will be able to refer to the domain name variable.

## Group variables

There are other cases where you want to set a variable that is valid for the whole group. Let's suppose that we want to declare the variable `https_enabled` to `True` and its value has to be equal for all web servers. In this case, we can create a `[webserver:vars]` section, so we will use the following `hosts` file:

```
[webserver]
ws01.fale.io
ws02.fale.io

[webserver:vars]
https_enabled=True

[database]
db01.fale.io
```

Remember that `host` variables will override `group` variables in case the same variable is declared in both spaces.

## Variable files

Sometimes, you have a lot of variables to declare for each `host` and `group`, and the `hosts` file gets hard to read. In those cases, you can move the variables to specific files. For host level variables, you'll need to create a file named the same as your host in the `host_vars` folder, while for `group` variables you'll have to use the group name for the file name and place them in the `group_vars` folder.

So, if we want to replicate the previous example of host-based variables using files, we will need to create the `host_vars/ws01.fale.io` file with the following content:

    domainname=example1.fale.io

Create the `host_vars/ws02.fale.io` file with the following content:

    domainname=example2.fale.io

While if we want to replicate the group based variables example, we will need to have the `group_vars/webserver` file with the following content:

    https_enabled=True

Inventory variables follow a hierarchy; at the top of this is the common variable file (we discussed this in the previous section, *Working with inventory files*) that will override any of the host variables, group variables, and inventory variable files. After this comes the host variables, which will override group variables; lastly, group variables will override inventory variable files.

## Overriding configuration parameters with an inventory file

You can override some of Ansible's configuration parameters directly through the inventory file. These configuration parameters will override all the other parameters that are set either through `ansible.cfg`, environment variables, or set in the playbooks themselves. Variable passed to the `ansible-playbook/ansible` command have priority over any other variable, including the ones set in the inventory file.

The following is the list of parameters you can override from an inventory file:

- `ansible_user`: This parameter is used to override the user that is used for communicating with the remote host. Sometimes, a certain machine needs a different user, in those cases this variable will help you.
- `ansible_port`: This parameter will override the default SSH port with the user-specified port. Sometimes sysadmin chooses to run SSH on a non-standard port. In this case, you'll need to instruct Ansible about the change.
- `ansible_host`: This parameter is used to override the host for an alias.
- `ansible_connection`: This specifies the connection type to the remote host. The values are SSH, Paramiko, or local.
- `ansible_private_key_file`: This parameter will override the private key used for SSH; this will be useful if you want to use specific keys for a specific host. A common use case is if you have hosts spread across multiple data centers, multiple AWS regions, or different kinds of applications. Private keys can potentially be different in such scenarios.
- `ansible__type`: By default, Ansible uses the **sh shell**; you can override this using the `ansible_shell_type` parameter. Changing this to `csh`, `ksh`, and so on will make Ansible use the commands of that shell.

# Working with dynamic inventory

There are environments where you have a system that creates and destroys machines automatically. We will see how to do this with Ansible in `Chapter 5`, *Going Cloud*. In such environments, the list of machines changes very quickly and keeping the `hosts` file becomes complicated. In this case, we can use dynamic inventories to solve the problem.

The idea behind dynamic inventories is that Ansible will not read the `hosts` file, but instead execute a script that will return the list of hosts to Ansible in JSON format. This allows you, for instance, to query your cloud provider and ask it directly, what machines in your entire infrastructure are running at any given moment.

Many scripts for the most common cloud providers are already present in Ansible at: `https://github.com/ansible/ansible/tree/devel/contrib/inventory` but you can create a custom script if you have different needs. The Ansible inventory scripts can be written in any language but, for consistency reasons, dynamic inventory scripts should be written in Python. Remember that these scripts need to be executable directly, so please remember to set them with the executable flag (`chmod + x inventory.py`).

*Scaling to Multiple Hosts*

In this chapter, we will take a look at Amazon Web Services and DigitalOcean scripts that can be downloaded from the official Ansible repository.

# Amazon Web Services

To allow Ansible to gather data from **Amazon Web Services** (**AWS**) about your EC2 instances, you need to download the following two files from Ansible's GitHub repository at `https://github.com/ansible/ansible`:

- The `ec2.py` inventory script
- The `ec2.ini` file, which contains the configuration for your EC2 inventory script

Ansible uses AWS Python library `boto` to communicate with AWS using APIs. To allow this communication, you need to export the `AWS_ACCESS_KEY_ID` and `AWS_SECRET_ACCESS_KEY` variables.

You can use the inventory in two ways:

- Pass it directly to an `ansible-playbook` command using the `-i` option and copy the `ec2.ini` file to your current directory where you are running the Ansible commands
- Copy the `ec2.py` file to `/etc/ansible/hosts`, make it executable using `chmod +x`, and copy the `ec2.ini` file to `/etc/ansible/ec2.ini`

The `ec2.py` file will create multiple groups based on the region, availability zone, tags, and so on. You can check the contents of the inventory file by running `./ec2.py --list`.

Let's see an example playbook with EC2 dynamic inventory, which will simply ping all machines in my account.

```
ansible -i ec2.py all -m ping
```

As expected, the two droplets I have on my account respond with the following:

```
52.28.138.231 | SUCCESS => {
    "changed": false,
    "ping": "pong"
}
```

In the preceding example, we're using the `ec2.py` script instead of a static inventory file with the `-i` option and the `ping` command.

Similarly, you can use these inventory scripts to perform various types of operations. For example, you can integrate it with your deployment script to figure out all the nodes in a single zone and deploy to them if you're performing your deployment zone-wise (a zone represents a data center) in AWS.

If you simply want to know what the web servers in the cloud are and you've tagged them using a certain convention, you can do that by using the dynamic inventory script by filtering out the tags. Furthermore, if you have special scenarios that are not covered by your present script, you can enhance it to provide the required set of nodes in JSON format and then act on those nodes from the playbooks. If you're using a database to manage your inventory, your inventory script can query the database and dump a JSON. It could even sync with your cloud and update your database on a regular basis.

# DigitalOcean

As we used the EC2 files in `https://github.com/ansible/ansible/tree/devel/contrib/inventory` to pull data from AWS, we can do the same for DigitalOcean. The only difference will be that we have to fetch the `digital_ocean.ini` and the `digital_ocean.py` files.

As before, we will need to tweak the `digital_ocean.ini` options, if needed and to make the Python file executable. The only option that you'll probably need to change is the `api_token`.

Now we can try to ping all machines available on `digital_ocean` with:

```
ansible -i digital_ocean.py all -m ping
```

As expected, the two droplets I have on my account respond with the following:

```
188.166.150.79 | SUCCESS => {
    "changed": false,
    "ping": "pong"
}
46.101.77.55 | SUCCESS => {
    "changed": false,
    "ping": "pong"
}
```

We have now seen how easy it is to retrieve data from many different cloud providers.

# Working with iterates in Ansible

You may have noticed that up to now we have never used cycles, so every time we had to do multiple, similar operations, we wrote the code multiple times. An example of this is the `webserver.yaml` code.

In fact, this was the content of the `webserver.yaml` file:

```
---
- hosts: webserver
  remote_user: ansible
  tasks:
  - name: Ensure the HTTPd package is installed
    yum:
      name: httpd
      state: present
    become: True
  - name: Ensure the HTTPd service is enabled and running
    service:
      name: httpd
      state: started
      enabled: True
    become: True
  - name: Ensure HTTP can pass the firewall
    firewalld:
      service: http
      state: enabled
      permanent: True
      immediate: True
    become: True
  - name: Ensure HTTPS can pass the firewall
    firewalld:
      service: https
      state: enabled
      permanent: True
      immediate: True
    become: True
```

As you can see, the last two blocks do the same operation (ensure that a certain port of the firewall is open).

# Standard iteration – with_items

To improve the above code, we can use a simple iteration: `with_items`.

This allows us to iterate in a list of item, and at every iteration, the designated item of the list will be available to us in the item variable.

We can therefore change that code to the following:

```
---
- hosts: webserver
  remote_user: ansible
  tasks:
  - name: Ensure the HTTPd package is installed
    yum:
      name: httpd
      state: present
    become: True
  - name: Ensure the HTTPd service is enabled and running
    service:
      name: httpd
      state: started
      enabled: True
    become: True
  - name: Ensure HTTP and HTTPS can pass the firewall
    firewalld:
      service: '{{ item }}'
      state: enabled
      permanent: True
      immediate: True
    become: True
    with_items:
    - http
    - https
```

We can execute it as the following:

```
ansible-playbook -i hosts webserver.yaml
```

We receive the following:

```
PLAY [webserver] *************************************************
TASK [setup] *****************************************************
ok: [ws01.fale.io]
ok: [ws02.fale.io]

TASK [Ensure the HTTPd package is installed] *********************
ok: [ws01.fale.io]
```

```
        ok: [ws02.fale.io]

        TASK [Ensure the HTTPd service is enabled and running] ***********
        ok: [ws02.fale.io]
        ok: [ws01.fale.io]

        TASK [Ensure HTTP can pass the firewall] ************************
        ok: [ws02.fale.io]
        ok: [ws01.fale.io]

        TASK [Ensure HTTP and HTTPS can pass the firewall] **************
        ok: [ws02.fale.io] => (item=http)
        ok: [ws01.fale.io] => (item=http)
        ok: [ws02.fale.io] => (item=https)
        ok: [ws01.fale.io] => (item=https)

        PLAY RECAP ******************************************************
        ws01.fale.io      : ok=5    changed=0    unreachable=0    failed=0
        ws02.fale.io      : ok=5    changed=0    unreachable=0    failed=0
```

As you can see, the output is slightly different from the previous execution, in fact on the lines for operations with loops we can see the item that was processed the "Ensure HTTP and HTTPS can pass the firewall" block

We have now seen that we can iterate on a list of items, but Ansible allows us other kind of iterations as well.

## Nested loops – with_nested

There are cases where you have to iterate all elements of a list with all items from other lists (**Cartesian product**). One case that is very common is when you have to create multiple folders in multiple paths. In our example, we will create the folders `mail` and `public_html` in the `home` folders of the users `alice` and `bob`.

We can do so with the following code from the `with_nested.yaml` file:

```
---
- hosts: all
  remote_user: ansible
  vars:
    users:
    - alice
    - bob
    folders:
    - mail
```

```yaml
      - public_html
    tasks:
    - name: Ensure the users exist
      user:
        name: '{{ item }}'
      become: True
      with_items:
      - '{{ users }}'
    - name: Ensure the folders exist
      file:
        path: '/home/{{ item.0 }}/{{ item.1 }}'
        state: directory
      become: True
      with_nested:
      - '{{ users }}'
      - '{{ folders }}'
```

Running this with the following:

```
ansible-playbook -i hosts with_nested.yaml
```

We receive the following result:

```
PLAY [all] *******************************************************
TASK [setup] *****************************************************
ok: [ws01.fale.io]
ok: [db01.fale.io]
ok: [ws02.fale.io]

TASK [Ensure the users exist] ************************************
changed: [db01.fale.io] => (item=alice)
changed: [ws01.fale.io] => (item=alice)
changed: [ws02.fale.io] => (item=alice)
changed: [db01.fale.io] => (item=bob)
changed: [ws01.fale.io] => (item=bob)
changed: [ws02.fale.io] => (item=bob)

TASK [Ensure the folders exist] **********************************
changed: [ws02.fale.io] => (item=[u'alice', u'mail'])
changed: [ws01.fale.io] => (item=[u'alice', u'mail'])
changed: [db01.fale.io] => (item=[u'alice', u'mail'])
changed: [ws01.fale.io] => (item=[u'alice', u'public_html'])
changed: [ws02.fale.io] => (item=[u'alice', u'public_html'])
changed: [db01.fale.io] => (item=[u'alice', u'public_html'])
changed: [ws02.fale.io] => (item=[u'bob', u'mail'])
changed: [ws01.fale.io] => (item=[u'bob', u'mail'])
changed: [db01.fale.io] => (item=[u'bob', u'mail'])
changed: [ws02.fale.io] => (item=[u'bob', u'public_html'])
```

*Scaling to Multiple Hosts*

```
changed: [ws01.fale.io] => (item=[u'bob', u'public_html'])
changed: [db01.fale.io] => (item=[u'bob', u'public_html'])

PLAY RECAP *********************************************************
db01.fale.io      : ok=3    changed=2    unreachable=0    failed=0
ws01.fale.io      : ok=3    changed=2    unreachable=0    failed=0
ws02.fale.io      : ok=3    changed=2    unreachable=0    failed=0
```

## Fileglobs loop – with_fileglobs

Sometimes, we want to do some kind of action on every file present in a certain folder. This could be handy if you want to copy multiple files with similar names from a folder to another. To do so, you can create a file called `with_fileglobs.yaml` with the following code:

```
---
- hosts: all
  remote_user: ansible
  tasks:
  - name: Ensure the folder /tmp/iproute2 is present
    file:
      dest: '/tmp/iproute2'
      state: directory
    become: True
  - name: Copy files that start with rt to the tmp folder
    copy:
      src: '{{ item }}'
      dest: '/tmp/iproute2'
      remote_src: True
    become: True
    with_fileglob:
    - '/etc/iproute2/rt_*'
```

We can execute it with the following:

```
ansible-playbook -i hosts with_fileglobs.yaml
```

To receive an output like the following:

```
PLAY [all] *********************************************************
TASK [setup] *******************************************************
ok: [ws02.fale.io]
ok: [db01.fale.io]
ok: [ws01.fale.io]

TASK [Ensure the folder /tmp/iproute2 is present] ***************
```

```
changed: [db01.fale.io]
changed: [ws01.fale.io]
changed: [ws02.fale.io]

TASK [Copy files that start with rt to the tmp folder] ***********
changed: [db01.fale.io] => (item=/etc/iproute2/rt_dsfield)
changed: [ws02.fale.io] => (item=/etc/iproute2/rt_dsfield)
changed: [ws01.fale.io] => (item=/etc/iproute2/rt_dsfield)
changed: [db01.fale.io] => (item=/etc/iproute2/rt_protos)
changed: [ws01.fale.io] => (item=/etc/iproute2/rt_protos)
changed: [ws02.fale.io] => (item=/etc/iproute2/rt_protos)
changed: [db01.fale.io] => (item=/etc/iproute2/rt_tables)
changed: [ws01.fale.io] => (item=/etc/iproute2/rt_tables)
changed: [ws02.fale.io] => (item=/etc/iproute2/rt_tables)
changed: [db01.fale.io] => (item=/etc/iproute2/rt_scopes)
changed: [ws01.fale.io] => (item=/etc/iproute2/rt_scopes)
changed: [ws02.fale.io] => (item=/etc/iproute2/rt_scopes)
changed: [db01.fale.io] => (item=/etc/iproute2/rt_realms)
changed: [ws01.fale.io] => (item=/etc/iproute2/rt_realms)
changed: [ws02.fale.io] => (item=/etc/iproute2/rt_realms)

PLAY RECAP *******************************************************
db01.fale.io         : ok=3    changed=2    unreachable=0    failed=0
ws01.fale.io         : ok=3    changed=2    unreachable=0    failed=0
ws02.fale.io         : ok=3    changed=2    unreachable=0    failed=0
```

# Integer loop – with_sequence

Many times you'll need to iterate over the integer numbers. An example could be to create ten folders called `fileXY`, where `XY` is the sequential numbers from `1` to `10`. To do so, we can create a file called `with_sequence.yaml` with the following code in it:

```
---
- hosts: all
  remote_user: ansible
  tasks:
  - name: Create the folders /tmp/dirXY with XY from 1 to 10
    file:
      dest: '/tmp/dir{{ item }}'
      state: directory
    with_sequence: start=1 end=10
    become: True
```

In the case of `with_sequence`, we must use the single line notation.

We can then execute it with:

```
ansible-playbook -i hosts with_sequence.yaml
```

We will receive:

```
PLAY [all] ************************************************************
TASK [setup] **********************************************************
ok: [db01.fale.io]
ok: [ws01.fale.io]
ok: [ws02.fale.io]

TASK [Create the folders /tmp/dirXY with XY from 1 to 10] ********
changed: [ws02.fale.io] => (item=1)
changed: [ws01.fale.io] => (item=1)
changed: [db01.fale.io] => (item=1)
changed: [db01.fale.io] => (item=2)
changed: [ws02.fale.io] => (item=2)
changed: [ws01.fale.io] => (item=2)
changed: [db01.fale.io] => (item=3)
changed: [ws01.fale.io] => (item=3)
changed: [ws02.fale.io] => (item=3)
changed: [db01.fale.io] => (item=4)
changed: [ws01.fale.io] => (item=4)
changed: [ws02.fale.io] => (item=4)
changed: [db01.fale.io] => (item=5)
changed: [ws01.fale.io] => (item=5)
changed: [ws02.fale.io] => (item=5)
changed: [db01.fale.io] => (item=6)
changed: [ws01.fale.io] => (item=6)
changed: [ws02.fale.io] => (item=6)
changed: [db01.fale.io] => (item=7)
changed: [ws01.fale.io] => (item=7)
changed: [ws02.fale.io] => (item=7)
changed: [db01.fale.io] => (item=8)
changed: [ws01.fale.io] => (item=8)
changed: [ws02.fale.io] => (item=8)
changed: [db01.fale.io] => (item=9)
changed: [ws01.fale.io] => (item=9)
changed: [ws02.fale.io] => (item=9)
changed: [db01.fale.io] => (item=10)
changed: [ws01.fale.io] => (item=10)
changed: [ws02.fale.io] => (item=10)
```

```
PLAY RECAP *************************************************
db01.fale.io              : ok=2     changed=1    unreachable=0    failed=0
ws01.fale.io              : ok=2     changed=1    unreachable=0    failed=0
ws02.fale.io              : ok=2     changed=1    unreachable=0    failed=0
```

Ansible supports many more types of loop, but since they are used far less, you can refer directly to the official documentation about loops at `http://docs.ansible.com/ansible/playbooks_loops.html`.

# Summary

In this chapter, we have seen a large number of concepts that will help scale your infrastructure beyond the single node. We started with inventories files used to instruct Ansible about our machines, then how to have host-specific and group-specific variables while running the same command on multiple heterogeneous hosts. We then moved on to dynamics inventories that are populated directly by some other system (usually a cloud provider). In the end, we analyzed multiple kinds of iteration in the Ansible playbooks.

In the next chapter, we will structure our Ansible files in a saner way to ensure maximum readability. To do this, we introduce roles which simplify the management of complex environments even more .

# 4
# Handling Complex Deployment

You must be wondering why the chapter is named the way it is. The reason for this is so far, we've not yet reached a stage where you can deploy the playbooks in production, especially in complex situations. Complex situations include those where you have to interact with several (hundred or thousand) machines where each group of machines is dependent on another group or groups of machines. These groups may be dependent on each other for all or some transactions, to perform secure complex data backups and replications with master and slaves. In addition, there are several interesting and rather compelling features of Ansible that we've not yet looked at. In this chapter, we will cover all of them with examples. Our aim is that, by the end of this chapter, you should have a clear idea of how to write playbooks that can be deployed in production from a configuration management perspective. The following chapters will add to what we've learned to enhance the experience of using Ansible.

To do so, we'll start with a feature that can come in handy for some occasions: the `local_action`.

# Working with the local_action feature

The `local_action` feature of Ansible is a powerful one, especially when we think of Orchestration. This feature allows you to run certain tasks locally on the machine that runs Ansible.

Consider the following situations:

- Spawning a new machine or creating a JIRA ticket
- Managing your command center(s) in terms of installing packages and setting up configurations
- Calling a load balancer API to disable a certain web server entry from the load balancer

These are tasks that can be run on the same machine that runs the `ansible-playbook` command rather than logging in to a remote box and running these commands.

Let's look at an example. Suppose you want to run a shell module on your local system where you are running your Ansible playbook. The `local_action` option comes into the picture in such situations. If you pass the module name and the module argument to `local_action`, it will run that module locally. Let's see how this option works with the `shell` module. Consider the following code that shows the output of the `local_action` option:

```
---
- hosts: database
  remote_user: ansible
  tasks:
  - name: Count processes running on the remote system
    shell: ps | wc -l
    register: remote_processes_number
  - name: Print remote running processes
    debug:
       msg: '{{ remote_processes_number.stdout }}'
  - name: Count processes running on the local system
    local_action: shell ps | wc -l
    register: local_processes_number
  - name: Print local running processes
    debug:
       msg: '{{ local_processes_number.stdout }}'
```

We can now save it as `local_action.yaml` and run it with the following:

```
ansible-playbook -i hosts local_action.yaml
```

We receive the following result:

```
PLAY [database] *******************************************************
TASK [setup] **********************************************************
ok: [db01.fale.io]

TASK [Count processes running on the remote system] **************
changed: [db01.fale.io]

TASK [Print remote running processes] ****************************
ok: [db01.fale.io] => {
    "msg": "7"
}

TASK [Count processes running on the local system] ***************
changed: [db01.fale.io -> localhost]

TASK [Print local running processes] *****************************
ok: [db01.fale.io] => {
    "msg": "11"
}

PLAY RECAP ************************************************************
db01.fale.io           : ok=5    changed=2    unreachable=0    failed=0
```

As you can see, the two commands provided us different numbers since they have been executed on different hosts. You can run any module with `local_action`, and Ansible will make sure that the module is run locally on the box where the `ansible-playbook` command is run. Another simple example you can (and should!) try is running two tasks:

- `uname` on the remote machine (`db01` in the preceding case)
- `uname` on the local machine but with local_action enabled

This will crystallize the idea of `local_action` further.

Ansible provides another method to delegate certain actions to a specific (or different) machine: the `delegate_to` system.

# Delegating a task

Sometimes you want to execute an action on a different system. This could be, for instance, a database node while you are deploying something on an application server node or to the local host. To do so, you can just add the `'delegate_to: HOST'` property to your task and it will be run on the proper node. Let's rework the previous example to achieve this:

```yaml
---
- hosts: database
  remote_user: ansible
  tasks:
  - name: Count processes running on the remote system
    shell: ps | wc -l
    register: remote_processes_number
  - name: Print remote running processes
    debug:
      msg: '{{ remote_processes_number.stdout }}'
  - name: Count processes running on the local system
    shell: ps | wc -l
    delegate_to: localhost
    register: local_processes_number
  - name: Print local running processes
    debug:
      msg: '{{ local_processes_number.stdout }}'
```

Saving it as `delegate_to.yaml`, we can run it with the following:

```
ansible-playbook -i hosts delegate_to.yaml
```

We will receive the same output as the previous example:

```
PLAY [database] ************************************************
TASK [setup] ***************************************************
ok: [db01.fale.io]

TASK [Count processes running on the remote system] **************
changed: [db01.fale.io]

TASK [Print remote running processes] ****************************
ok: [db01.fale.io] => {
    "msg": "7"
}

TASK [Count processes running on the local system] ***************
changed: [db01.fale.io -> localhost]

TASK [Print local running processes] *****************************
ok: [db01.fale.io] => {
    "msg": "11"
}

PLAY RECAP *****************************************************
db01.fale.io        : ok=5    changed=2    unreachable=0    failed=0
```

# Working with conditionals

Until now, we have only seen how playbooks work and how tasks are executed. We also saw that Ansible executes all these tasks sequentially. However, this would not help you while writing an advanced playbook that contains tens of tasks and have to execute only a subset of these tasks. For example, let's say you have a playbook that will install Apache HTTPd server on the remote host. Now, the Apache HTTPd server has a different package name for a Debian-based operating system, and it's called `apache2`; for a Red-Hat-based operating system, it's called `httpd`.

Having two tasks, one for the `httpd` package (for Red-Hat-based systems) and the other for the `apache2` package (for Debian-based systems) in a playbook, will make Ansible install both packages, and this execution will fail, as `apache2` will not be available if you're installing on a Red-Hat-based operating system. To overcome such problems, Ansible provides conditional statements that help run a task only when a specified condition is met. In this case, we do something similar to the following pseudocode:

```
If os = "redhat"
   Install httpd
Else if os = "debian"
   Install apache2
End
```

While installing `httpd` on a Red-Hat-based operating system, we first check whether the remote system is running a Red-Hat-based operating system, and if it is, we then install the `httpd` package; otherwise, we skip the task. Without wasting your time, let's dive into an example playbook called `conditional_httpd.yaml` with the following content:

```
---
- hosts: webserver
  remote_user: ansible
  tasks:
  - name: Print the ansible_os_family value
    debug:
      msg: '{{ ansible_os_family }}'
  - name: Ensure the httpd package is updated
    yum:
      name: httpd
      state: latest
    become: True
    when: ansible_os_family == 'RedHat'
  - name: Ensure the apache2 package is updated
    apt:
      name: apache2
      state: latest
```

```
      become: True
      when: ansible_os_family == 'Debian'
```

Run it with the following:

```
ansible-playbook -i hosts conditional_httpd.yaml
```

This is the result:

```
PLAY [webserver] *********************************************
TASK [setup] *************************************************
ok: [ws03.fale.io]
ok: [ws01.fale.io]
ok: [ws02.fale.io]

TASK [Print the ansible_os_family value] *********************
ok: [ws01.fale.io] => {
    "msg": "RedHat"
}
ok: [ws02.fale.io] => {
    "msg": "RedHat"
}
ok: [ws03.fale.io] => {
    "msg": "Debian"
}

TASK [Ensure the httpd package is updated] *******************
skipping: [ws03.fale.io]
changed: [ws01.fale.io]
changed: [ws02.fale.io]

TASK [Ensure the apache2 package is updated] *****************
skipping: [ws02.fale.io]
skipping: [ws01.fale.io]
changed: [ws03.fale.io]

PLAY RECAP ***************************************************
ws01.fale.io        : ok=3    changed=1    unreachable=0    failed=0
ws02.fale.io        : ok=3    changed=1    unreachable=0    failed=0
ws03.fale.io        : ok=3    changed=1    unreachable=0    failed=0
```

As you can see, I've created a new server (ws03) for this example that is Debian-based. As expected, the installation of the httpd package was performed on the two CentOS nodes, while the installation of the apache2 package was performed on the Debian node.

Ansible only distinguishes between a few families (AIX, Alpine, Altlinux, Archlinux, Darwin, Debian, FreeBSD, Gentoo, HP-UX, Mandrake, Red Hat, Slackware, Solaris, and Suse at the time of writing this book), for this reason a CentOS machine has an `ansible_os_family` value; 'RedHat'.

Likewise, you can match for different conditions as well. Ansible supports equal to (==), different than (!=), bigger than (>), smaller than (<), bigger than or equal to (>-), and smaller than or equal to (<=).

The operators we have seen so far will match the entire content of the variable, but what if you just want to check whether a particular character or a string is present in a variable? To perform these kinds of checks, Ansible provides the in and not operators. You can also match multiple conditions using the AND and OR operators. The AND operator will make sure that all conditions are matched before executing this task, whereas the OR operator will make sure that at least one of the conditions there is a match for at least one of the conditions, for example, you can use `foo >= 0 and foo <= 5`.

## Boolean conditionals

Apart from string matching, you can also check whether a variable is True. This type of validation will be useful when you want to check whether a variable was assigned a value or not. You can even execute a task based on the Boolean value of a variable.

For example, let's put the following code in a file called `crontab_backup.yaml`:

```yaml
---
- hosts: all
  remote_user: ansible
  vars:
    backup: True
  tasks:
  - name: Copy the crontab in tmp if the backup variable is true
    copy:
      src: /etc/crontab
      dest: /tmp/crontab
      remote_src: True
    when: backup
```

If we execute it with the following:

```
ansible-playbook -i hosts crontab_backup.yaml
```

We will obtain the following:

```
PLAY [all] *************************************************************
TASK [setup] ***********************************************************
ok: [db01.fale.io]
ok: [ws02.fale.io]
ok: [ws01.fale.io]

TASK [Copy the crontab in tmp if the backup variable is true] ****
changed: [ws02.fale.io]
changed: [db01.fale.io]
changed: [ws01.fale.io]

PLAY RECAP *************************************************************
db01.fale.io               : ok=2    changed=1    unreachable=0    failed=0
ws01.fale.io               : ok=2    changed=1    unreachable=0    failed=0
ws02.fale.io               : ok=2    changed=1    unreachable=0    failed=0
```

But if we change the command slightly, to:

```
ansible-playbook -i hosts crontab_backup.yaml --extra-vars="backup=False"
```

We will receive this output:

```
PLAY [all] *************************************************************
TASK [setup] ***********************************************************
ok: [db01.fale.io]
ok: [ws02.fale.io]
ok: [ws01.fale.io]

TASK [Copy the crontab in tmp if the backup variable is true] ****
skipping: [ws01.fale.io]
skipping: [ws02.fale.io]
skipping: [db01.fale.io]

PLAY RECAP *************************************************************
db01.fale.io               : ok=1    changed=0    unreachable=0    failed=0
ws01.fale.io               : ok=1    changed=0    unreachable=0    failed=0
ws02.fale.io               : ok=1    changed=0    unreachable=0    failed=0
```

As you can see, in the first case the operation has been executed, while in the second case it was skipped. We could have overwritten the backup value using a configuration file, a `host` variable, or a `group` variable.

If checked in this way and if the variable is not set, Ansible will assume it to be `False`.

## Checking if a variable is set

Sometimes you find yourself having to use a variable in a command. Every time you do so, you have to ensure that the variable is *set*. This is because some commands could be catastrophic if called with an *unset* variable (that is: if you execute `rm -rf $VAR/*` and `$VAR` is not set or empty, it will nuke your machine). To do so, Ansible provides a way to check whether a variable is defined or not.

We could improve the previous example in the following way:

```
---
- hosts: all
  remote_user: ansible
  vars:
    backup: True
  tasks:
  - name: Check if the backup_folder is set
    fail:
      msg: 'The backup_folder needs to be set'
    when: backup_folder is not defined
  - name: Copy the crontab in tmp if the backup variable is true
    copy:
      src: /etc/crontab
      dest: '{{ backup_folder }}/crontab'
      remote_src: True
    when: backup
```

As you can see, we have used the `fail` module that allows us to put the Ansible playbook in a failure state in case the `backup_folder` variable is not set.

## Working with include

The `include` feature helps you to reduce duplicity while writing tasks. This also allows us to have smaller playbooks by including reusable code in separate tasks using the **Don't Repeat Yourself** (**DRY**) principle.

To trigger the inclusion of another file, you need to put the following under the tasks object:

```
- include: FILENAME.yaml
```

You can also pass some variables to the included file. To do so, we can specify them in the following way:

```
- include: FILENAME.yaml variable1="value1" variable2="value2"
```

In addition of passing variables, you can also use conditionals to include a file only when certain conditions are matched, for instance to include the `redhat.yaml` file only if the machine is running an OS in the Red Hat family using the following code:

```
- name: Include the file only for Red Hat OSes
  include: redhat.yaml
  when: ansible_os_family == "RedHat"
```

# Working with handlers

In many situations, you will have a task or a group of tasks that change certain resources on the remote machines, which need to trigger an event to become effective. For example, when you change a service configuration, you will need to restart or reload the service itself. In Ansible you can trigger this event using the `notify` action.

Every handler task will run at the end of the playbook if notified. For example, you changed your HTTPd server configuration multiple times and you want to restart the HTTPd service so that the changes are applied. Now, restarting HTTPd every single time you make a configuration change is not a good practice; it is not a good practice to restart the server even if no changes has been made to its configurations. To deal with such a situation, you can notify Ansible to restart the HTTPd service on every configuration change, but Ansible will make sure that no matter how many times you notify it for the HTTPd restart, it will call that task just once after all other tasks complete. Let's change the `webserver.yaml` file we created in the previous chapters a little bit, in the following way:

```
---
- hosts: webserver
  remote_user: ansible
  tasks:
  - name: Ensure the HTTPd package is installed
    yum:
       name: httpd
       state: present
    become: True
  - name: Ensure the HTTPd service is enabled and running
```

```yaml
      service:
        name: httpd
        state: started
        enabled: True
      become: True
    - name: Ensure HTTP can pass the firewall
      firewalld:
        service: http
        state: enabled
        permanent: True
        immediate: True
      become: True
    - name: Ensure HTTPd configuration is updated
      copy:
        src: website.conf
        dest: /etc/httpd/conf.d
      become: True
      notify: Restart HTTPd
  handlers:
    - name: Restart HTTPd
      service:
        name: httpd
        state: restarted
      become: True
```

Run this script with:

```
ansible-playbook -i hosts webserver.yaml
```

We will have the following output:

```
PLAY [webserver] *********************************************
TASK [setup] *************************************************
ok: [ws01.fale.io]
ok: [ws02.fale.io]

TASK [Ensure the HTTPd package is installed] *****************
ok: [ws02.fale.io]
ok: [ws01.fale.io]

TASK [Ensure the HTTPd service is enabled and running] **********
ok: [ws02.fale.io]
ok: [ws01.fale.io]

TASK [Ensure HTTP can pass the firewall] *************************
ok: [ws02.fale.io]
ok: [ws01.fale.io]
```

```
TASK [Ensure HTTPd configuration is updated] ********************
changed: [ws02.fale.io]
changed: [ws01.fale.io]

RUNNING HANDLER [Restart HTTPd] *********************************
changed: [ws02.fale.io]
changed: [ws01.fale.io]

PLAY RECAP ******************************************************
ws01.fale.io      : ok=6    changed=2    unreachable=0    failed=0
ws02.fale.io      : ok=6    changed=2    unreachable=0    failed=0
```

In this case, the handler has been triggered from the configuration file change. But if we run it a second time, the configuration will not change and therefore we will have the following result:

```
PLAY [webserver] ************************************************
TASK [setup] ****************************************************
ok: [ws01.fale.io]
ok: [ws02.fale.io]

TASK [Ensure the HTTPd package is installed] ********************
ok: [ws02.fale.io]
ok: [ws01.fale.io]

TASK [Ensure the HTTPd service is enabled and running] **********
ok: [ws02.fale.io]
ok: [ws01.fale.io]

TASK [Ensure HTTP can pass the firewall] ************************
ok: [ws01.fale.io]
ok: [ws02.fale.io]

TASK [Ensure HTTPd configuration is updated] ********************
ok: [ws02.fale.io]
ok: [ws01.fale.io]

PLAY RECAP ******************************************************
ws01.fale.io      : ok=5    changed=0    unreachable=0    failed=0
ws02.fale.io      : ok=5    changed=0    unreachable=0    failed=0
```

When using handlers, those are triggered only a single time, even if they are called multiple times during the playbook execution. By default, handlers are executed at the end of the playbook execution, but you can force them to be run when you want using the meta task with the flush_handlers option like: - meta: flush_handlers

# Working with roles

We have seen how we can automate simple tasks, but what we have seen up till now will not solve all your problems. This is because playbooks are very good at executing operations, but are not very good for configuring huge amounts of machines, because they will soon become messy. To solve this, Ansible has roles.

My definition of a role is a set of playbooks, templates, files, or variables to achieve a specific goal. For instance, we could have a database role and a web server role so that those configurations stay cleanly separated.

Before starting to look inside a role, let's talk about a project organization.

# Project organization

In the last few years, I've worked on multiple Ansible repositories for multiple organizations and many of them were very chaotic. To ensure that your repository is easy to manage, I'm going to give you a template that I always use.

First of all, I always create three files in the `root` folder:

- `ansible.cfg`: A small configuration file to explain to Ansible where to find the files in our folder structure
- `hosts`: The hosts file we have already seen in the previous chapters
- `master.yaml`: A playbook that aligns the whole infrastructure

In addition to those three files, I create two folders:

- `playbooks`: This will contain the playbooks and a folder called *groups* for groups management
- `roles`: This will contain all the roles we need

To clarify this, let's use the Linux `tree` command to see the structure of an Ansible repository for a simple web application needing web servers and database servers:

```
ansible.cfg
hosts
master.yaml
playbooks
    firstrun.yaml
    groups
        database.yaml
        webserver.yaml
roles
    common
    database
    webserver
```

As you can see, I've added a `common` role as well. This is very useful for putting in all the things that should be performed for every server. Usually, I configure NTP, motd, and other similar services in this role, as well as the machine hostname.

We will now see how to structure a role.

# Anatomy of a role

The structure of folders in a role is standard and you cannot change it much.

The most important folder within the role is the `tasks` folder because this is the only mandatory folder in it. It has to contain a `main.yaml` file that will be the list of tasks to be executed. Other folders that are often present in the roles are templates and files. The first one will be used to store templates used by the **template task**, while the second will be used to store files that are used by the **copy task**.

# Transforming your playbooks in a full Ansible project

Let's see how to transform the three playbooks we used to set up our web infrastructure (`common_tasks.yaml`, `firstrun.yaml`, and `webserver.yaml`) to fit this file organization. We have to remember that we also used two files (`index.html.j2` and `motd`) in those roles, so we have to place these files properly too.

First, we are going to create the folder structure we have seen in the previous paragraph.

The easiest playbook to port is the `firstrun.yaml` since we only need to copy it into the playbooks folder. This playbook will remain a playbook because it's a set of operations that will have to be run just one time for each server.

We now move to the `common_tasks.yaml` playbook, which will need a little bit of rework to match the role paradigm.

## Transforming a playbook into a role

The first thing we need is to create the `roles/common/tasks` and `roles/common/templates` folders. In the first one we will add the following `main.yaml` file:

```
---
- name: Ensure EPEL is enabled
  yum:
    name: epel-release
    state: present
  become: True
- name: Ensure libselinux-python is present
  yum:
    name: libselinux-python
    state: present
  become: True
- name: Ensure libsemanage-python is present
  yum:
    name: libsemanage-python
    state: present
  become: True
- name: Ensure we have last version of every package
  yum:
    name: "*"
    state: latest
  become: True
- name: Ensure NTP is installed
  yum:
    name: ntp
    state: present
  become: True
- name: Ensure the timezone is set to UTC
  file:
    src: /usr/share/zoneinfo/GMT
    dest: /etc/localtime
    state: link
```

## Handling Complex Deployment

```yaml
      become: True
    - name: Ensure the NTP service is running and enabled
      service:
        name: ntpd
        state: started
        enabled: True
      become: True
    - name: Ensure FirewallD is installed
      yum:
        name: firewalld
        state: present
      become: True
    - name: Ensure FirewallD is running
      service:
        name: firewalld
        state: started
        enabled: True
      become: True
    - name: Ensure SSH can pass the firewall
      firewalld:
        service: ssh
        state: enabled
        permanent: True
        immediate: True
      become: True
    - name: Ensure the MOTD file is present and updated
      template:
        src: motd
        dest: /etc/motd
        owner: root
        group: root
        mode: 0644
      become: True
    - name: Ensure the hostname is the same of the inventory
      hostname:
        name: "{{ inventory_hostname }}"
      become: True
```

As you can see, this is very similar to our `common_tasks.yaml` playbooks. In fact, there are only two differences:

- The lines; `hosts`, `remote_user`, and `tasks` (lines 2,3, and 4) have been deleted
- The indentation of the rest of the file has been fixed accordingly

In this role, we used the template task to create a `motd` file on the server with the IP of the machine and other interesting information. For this reason, we need to create `roles/common/templates` and put the `motd` template in it.

At this point, our common task will have this structure:

```
common/
    tasks
        main.yaml
    templates
        motd
```

We now need to instruct Ansible on the machines that will need to perform all the tasks specified in the `common` role. To do so, we should look at the `playbooks/groups` directory. In this directory, it is handy to have one file for each group of logically similar machines (that is, machines that are performing the same kind of operation). In our case, database and web server.

So, let's create a `database.yaml` file in `playbooks/groups` with the following content:

```
---
- hosts: database
  user: ansible
  roles:
    - common
```

Create a `webserver.yaml` file in the same folder with the following content:

```
---
- hosts: webserver
  user: ansible
  roles:
    - common
```

As you can see, those files specify the group of hosts that we want to operate on, the remote user to use on those hosts, and the roles that we want to execute.

## Helper files

When we created the `hosts` file in the previous chapter, we noticed that it helps to simplify our command lines. So, let's start copying the hosts files we previously used in the `root` folder of our Ansible repository. Up to now, we have always specified the path of this file on the command line. This is no longer necessary if we create an `ansible.cfg` file that tells Ansible the location of our `hosts` file. For this reason, let's create an `ansible.cfg` file in the root of our Ansible repository with the following content:

```
[defaults]
hostfile = hosts
host_key_checking = False
roles_path = roles
```

In this file, we have also specified another two variables in addition to the `hostfile` one that we already talk about, and those are `host_key_checking` and `roles_path`.

The `host_key_checking` flag is useful to not require the verification of the remote system SSH key. This is not suggested for use in production, since the usage of a public key propagation system is suggested for such environments, but is very handy in testing environments since it will help you to reduce the time Ansible hangs waiting for user input.

The `roles_path` is used to tell Ansible where to find the roles for our playbooks.

I usually add one additional file, which is `master.yaml`. I find it very useful as you will often need to keep your infrastructure aligned with your Ansible code. To do it in a single command, you'll need a file that will run all of the files in `playbooks/groups`. So, let's create a `master.yaml` file in the Ansible repository `root` folder with the following content:

```
---
- include: playbooks/groups/database.yaml
- include: playbooks/groups/webserver.yaml
```

At this point, we can execute the following:

**ansible-playbook master.yaml**

The result will be the following:

```
PLAY [database] *************************************************
TASK [setup] ****************************************************
ok: [db01.fale.io]

TASK [common : Ensure EPEL is enabled] **************************
ok: [db01.fale.io]
```

```
TASK [common : Ensure libselinux-python is present] **************
ok: [db01.fale.io]

TASK [common : Ensure libsemanage-python is present] *************
ok: [db01.fale.io]

TASK [common : Ensure we have last version of every package] *****
changed: [db01.fale.io]

TASK [common : Ensure NTP is installed] **************************
ok: [db01.fale.io]

TASK [common : Ensure the timezone is set to UTC] ****************
ok: [db01.fale.io]

TASK [common : Ensure the NTP service is running and enabled] ****
ok: [db01.fale.io]

TASK [common : Ensure FirewallD is installed] ********************
ok: [db01.fale.io]

TASK [common : Ensure FirewallD is running] **********************
ok: [db01.fale.io]

TASK [common : Ensure SSH can pass the firewall] *****************
ok: [db01.fale.io]

TASK [common : Ensure the MOTD file is present and updated] ******
ok: [db01.fale.io]

TASK [common : Ensure the hostname is the same of the inventory] *
ok: [db01.fale.io]

PLAY [webserver] *************************************************
TASK [setup] *****************************************************
ok: [ws01.fale.io]
ok: [ws02.fale.io]

TASK [common : Ensure EPEL is enabled] ***************************
ok: [ws01.fale.io]
ok: [ws02.fale.io]

TASK [common : Ensure libselinux-python is present] **************
ok: [ws02.fale.io]
ok: [ws01.fale.io]

TASK [common : Ensure libsemanage-python is present] *************
ok: [ws01.fale.io]
```

```
ok: [ws02.fale.io]

TASK [common : Ensure we have last version of every package] *****
changed: [ws01.fale.io]
changed: [ws02.fale.io]

TASK [common : Ensure NTP is installed] *************************
ok: [ws01.fale.io]
ok: [ws02.fale.io]

TASK [common : Ensure the timezone is set to UTC] ***************
ok: [ws01.fale.io]
ok: [ws02.fale.io]

TASK [common : Ensure the NTP service is running and enabled] ****
ok: [ws02.fale.io]
ok: [ws01.fale.io]

TASK [common : Ensure FirewallD is installed] *******************
ok: [ws02.fale.io]
ok: [ws01.fale.io]

TASK [common : Ensure FirewallD is running] *********************
ok: [ws01.fale.io]
ok: [ws02.fale.io]

TASK [common : Ensure SSH can pass the firewall] ****************
ok: [ws01.fale.io]
ok: [ws02.fale.io]

TASK [common : Ensure the MOTD file is present and updated] ******
ok: [ws01.fale.io]
ok: [ws02.fale.io]

TASK [common : Ensure the hostname is the same of the inventory] *
ok: [ws02.fale.io]
ok: [ws01.fale.io]

PLAY RECAP *******************************************************
db01.fale.io     : ok=13    changed=1    unreachable=0    failed=0
ws01.fale.io     : ok=13    changed=1    unreachable=0    failed=0
ws02.fale.io     : ok=13    changed=1    unreachable=0    failed=0
```

As you can see, the actions listed in the `common` role have been executed on the node in the `database` group first and then on the nodes in the `webserver` group.

## Transforming the webserver role

As we transformed the `common` playbook into the `common` role, we can do the same for the `webserver` role.

In roles, we need to have the `webserver` folder with the `tasks` subfolder inside it. In this folder, we have to put the `main.yaml` file containing the `tasks` copied from the playbooks, that should look like:

```yaml
---
- name: Ensure the HTTPd package is installed
  yum:
    name: httpd
    state: present
  become: True
- name: Ensure the HTTPd service is enabled and running
  service:
    name: httpd
    state: started
    enabled: True
  become: True
- name: Ensure HTTP can pass the firewall
  firewalld:
    service: http
    state: enabled
    permanent: True
    immediate: True
  become: True
- name: Ensure HTTPd configuration is updated
  copy:
    src: website.conf
    dest: /etc/httpd/conf.d
  become: True
  notify: Restart HTTPd
- name: Ensure the website is present and updated
  template:
    src: index.html.j2
    dest: /var/www/html/index.html
    owner: root
    group: root
    mode: 0644
  become: True
```

# Handling Complex Deployment

In this role, we have used multiple tasks that will need additional resources to work properly, more specifically we need to:

- Put the `website.conf` file in `roles/webserver/files`
- Put the `index.html.j2` template in `roles/webserver/templates`
- Create the `Restart HTTPd` handler

The first two should be pretty straightforward. The first one, in fact, is an empty file (we have not yet put anything in it since the default configuration was good enough for our use) and the `index.html.j2` file should contain the following content:

```
<html>
    <body>
        <h1>Hello World!</h1>
        <p>This page was created on {{ ansible_date_time.date }}.</p>
        <p>This machine can be reached on the following IP addresses</p>
        <ul>
{% for address in ansible_all_ipv4_addresses %}
            <li>{{ address }}</li>
{% endfor %}
        </ul>
    </body>
</html>
```

## Handlers in roles

The last thing we need to do to complete this role is to create the handler for the `Restart HTTPd` notification. To do so, we will need to create a `main.yaml` file in `roles/webserver/handlers` with the following content:

```
---
- name: Restart HTTPd
  service:
    name: httpd
    state: restarted
  become: True
```

As you may notice, this is very similar to the handler we used in the playbook if not for the file location and indentation.

*Chapter 4*

The only thing that we still need to do to make our role applicable is to add the entry in the `playbooks/groups/webserver.yaml` file so that Ansible is informed that the servers in the `webserver` group should apply the `webserver` role as well as the common role. Our `playbooks/groups/webserver.yaml` will need to be like the following:

```
---
- hosts: webserver
  user: ansible
  roles:
  - common
  - webserver
```

We could now execute the `master.yaml` again to apply the `webserver` role to the relevant servers, but we can also just execute the `playbooks/groups/webserver.yaml`, since the change we just did is relevant only to this group of servers. To do so we run:

**ansible-playbook playbooks/groups/webserver.yaml**

We should receive an output similar to the following:

```
PLAY [webserver] ***********************************************
TASK [setup] ***************************************************
ok: [ws02.fale.io]
ok: [ws01.fale.io]

TASK [common : Ensure EPEL is enabled] *************************
ok: [ws01.fale.io]
ok: [ws02.fale.io]

TASK [common : Ensure libselinux-python is present] ************
ok: [ws01.fale.io]
ok: [ws02.fale.io]

TASK [common : Ensure libsemanage-python is present] ***********
ok: [ws01.fale.io]
ok: [ws02.fale.io]

TASK [common : Ensure we have last version of every package] *****
ok: [ws01.fale.io]
ok: [ws02.fale.io]

TASK [common : Ensure NTP is installed] ************************
ok: [ws02.fale.io]
ok: [ws01.fale.io]

TASK [common : Ensure the timezone is set to UTC] **************
ok: [ws01.fale.io]
```

```
ok: [ws02.fale.io]

TASK [common : Ensure the NTP service is running and enabled] ****
ok: [ws01.fale.io]
ok: [ws02.fale.io]

TASK [common : Ensure FirewallD is installed] ********************
ok: [ws01.fale.io]
ok: [ws02.fale.io]

TASK [common : Ensure FirewallD is running] **********************
ok: [ws02.fale.io]
ok: [ws01.fale.io]

TASK [common : Ensure SSH can pass the firewall] *****************
ok: [ws01.fale.io]
ok: [ws02.fale.io]

TASK [common : Ensure the MOTD file is present and updated] ******
ok: [ws01.fale.io]
ok: [ws02.fale.io]

TASK [common : Ensure the hostname is the same of the inventory] *
ok: [ws02.fale.io]
ok: [ws01.fale.io]

TASK [webserver : Ensure the HTTPd package is installed] *********
ok: [ws01.fale.io]
ok: [ws02.fale.io]

TASK [webserver : Ensure the HTTPd service is enabled and running]
ok: [ws01.fale.io]
ok: [ws02.fale.io]

TASK [webserver : Ensure HTTP can pass the firewall] *************
ok: [ws02.fale.io]
ok: [ws01.fale.io]

TASK [webserver : Ensure HTTPd configuration is updated] *********
ok: [ws01.fale.io]
ok: [ws02.fale.io]

TASK [webserver : Ensure the website is present and updated] *****
changed: [ws01.fale.io]
changed: [ws02.fale.io]

PLAY RECAP *******************************************************
ws01.fale.io               : ok=18    changed=1    unreachable=0    failed=0
```

```
ws02.fale.io        : ok=18    changed=1   unreachable=0   failed=0
```

As you can see, both the `common` and the `webserver` roles has been applied to the `webserver` nodes.

It's very important to apply all roles concerning a specific node and not just the one you changed because more often than not, when there is a problem on one or more nodes in a group but not on other nodes of the same group, the problem is some roles have been applied unequally in the group. Only by applying all concerned roles to a group, will it grant you the equality of the nodes of that group.

# Execution strategies

Before Ansible 2, every task needed to be executed (and completed) on each machine before Ansible issued a new task to all machines. This meant that if you are performing tasks on a hundred machines and one of them is under-performing, all machines will go at the under-performing machine's speed.

With Ansible 2, the execution strategies have been made modular and therefore you can now choose which execution strategy you prefer for your playbooks. You can also write custom execution strategies, but this is beyond the scope of this book. At the moment (in Ansible 2.1) there are only three execution strategies: **linear**, **serial**, and **free**:

- **Linear execution**: This strategy behaves exactly as Ansible did prior to version 2. This is the default strategy.

- **Serial execution**: This strategy will take a subset of hosts (the default is five) and execute all tasks against those hosts before moving to the next subset and starting from the beginning. This kind of execution strategy could help you to work on a limited number of hosts so that you always have some hosts that are available to your users. If you are looking for this kind of deployment, you will need a load balancer in front of your hosts that needs to be informed about which nodes are in maintenance at every given moment.

- **Free execution**: This strategy will serve a new task to each host as soon as that host has completed the previous task. This will allow faster hosts to complete the playbook before slower nodes. If you choose this execution strategy you have to remember that some tasks could require a previous task to be completed on all nodes (for instance, clustering databases require all database nodes to have the database installed and running) and in this case they will probably fail.

# Tasks blocks

In Ansible 2.0 blocks have been made available. Blocks allow you to group tasks in a logical way and they can also help for a better error handling.
The majority of properties you can add to a standard task, you can also add it to the blocks. You may need to perform a yum task to install NTPd and enable of the service only if the machine is CentOS. To do so, the following code can be used:

```
tasks:
- block:
    - name: Ensure NTPd is present
      yum:
        name: ntpd
        state: present
    - name: Ensure NTPd is running
      service:
        name: ntpd
        state: started
        enabled: True
  when: ansible_distribution == 'CentOS'
```

As you can notice, the when clause has been applied to the block so all tasks within the block will be performed only if the when clause will be true.

# The Ansible template – Jinja filters

We have seen in the second chapter that templates allow you to dynamically complete your playbook and place files on servers based on dynamic data such as `host` and `group` variables. In this section, we will move forward and see how Jinja2 filters work with Ansible.

Jinja2 filters are simple Python functions that take some arguments, process them, and return the result. For example, consider the following command:

```
{{ myvar | filter }}
```

In the preceding example, `myvar` is a variable; Ansible will pass `myvar` to the Jinja2 filter as an argument. The Jinja2 filter will then process it and return the resulting data. Jinja2 filters even acccpt additional arguments as follows:

```
{{ myvar | filter(2) }}
```

In this example, Ansible will now pass two arguments, that is, `myvar` and 2. Likewise, you can pass multiple arguments to filters separated by commas.

Ansible supports a wide variety of Jinja2 filters, we will see some of the important Jinja2 filters that you might need to use while writing your playbook.

## Formatting data using filters

Ansible supports Jinja2 filters to format data to JSON or YAML. You pass a dictionary variable to this filter, and it will format your data into JSON or YAML. For example, consider the following command-line:

```
{{ users | to_nice_json }}
```

In the preceding example, `users` is the variable and `to_nice_json` is the Jinja2 filter. As we saw earlier, Ansible will internally pass `users` as an argument to the Jinja2 filter `to_nice_json`. Likewise, you can format your data into YAML as well by using the following command:

```
{{ users | to_nice_yaml }}
```

## Using filters with conditionals

You can use Jinja2 filters with conditionals for checking if the status of a task is failed, changed, success, or skipped. Let's start creating a file in our `playbooks` folder with the following content:

```
---
- hosts: webserver
  remote_user: ansible
  tasks:
  - name: Checking HTTPd service status
    service:
      name: httpd
      state: running
    register: httpd_result
    ignore_errors: true
  - debug:
      msg: Previous task failed
    when: httpd_result|failed
```

In the preceding example, we first checked whether the `httpd` service was running and stored the output of that module in the `httpd_result` variable. We then checked whether the previous task failed using the Jinja2 filter, `httpd_result|failed`. Ansible will skip this task if the when condition fails, that is, if the previous task passed. Likewise, you can use changed, success, or skipped filters.

We can now check that the previous `playbook` executed as expected, running it as:

```
ansible-playbook playbooks/http_status.yaml
```

I've stopped HTTPd on the `ws01.fale.io` server with the command, `systemctl stop httpd` and running it will give me the following result:

```
PLAY [webserver] ***********************************************
TASK [setup] ***************************************************
ok: [ws02.fale.io]
ok: [ws01.fale.io]

TASK [Checking HTTPd service status] ***************************
ok: [ws02.fale.io]
fatal: [ws01.fale.io]: FAILED! => {"changed": false, "failed": true, "msg": "Failed to start httpd.service: Interactive authentication required.\n"}
...ignoring

TASK [debug] ***************************************************
skipping: [ws02.fale.io]
```

```
ok: [ws01.fale.io] => {
    "msg": "Previous task failed"
}

PLAY RECAP *********************************************************
ws01.fale.io              : ok=3    changed=0    unreachable=0    failed=0
ws02.fale.io              : ok=2    changed=0    unreachable=0    failed=0
```

# Defaulting undefined variables

We have seen in the previous sections, that it is always wise to check if a variable is defined before using it. We can set a `default` value for the variable so that instead of failing, Ansible will use that value if the variable is not defined. To do so, we use:

`{{ backup_disk | default("/dev/sdf") }}`

This filter will not assign the `default` value to the variable; it will only pass the `default` value to the current task where it is being used. Let's look at a few more examples of Jinja filters themselves before closing this section:

Using random number filters: To find a random number, character, or string out of a list, you can use the random filter:

- Execute this to get a random character from a list:

    `{{['a', 'b', 'c', 'd'] | random}}`

- Execute this to get a random number from 0 to 100:

    `{{100 | random}}`

- Execute this to get a random number from 10 to 50:

    `{{50 | random(10)}}`

- Execute this to get a random number from 20 to 50 in steps of 10:

    `{{50 | random(20, 10)}}`

Concatenating a list to the string using filters: Jinja2 filters allow you to concatenate a list to a string using the join filter. This filter takes a separator as an extra argument. If you do not specify a separator, then the filter will combine all elements of the list together without any separation. Consider the following example:

`{{["This", "is", "a", "string"] | join(" ")}}`

*Handling Complex Deployment*

- The preceding filter will result in a This is a string output. You can specify any separator you want instead of a white space.

- Encoding or decoding data using filters: You can encode or decode data using filters as follows:

- Encode your data to `base64` using the `b64encode` filter:

   **{{variable | b64encode}}**

- Decode an encoded `base64` string using the `b64decode` filter:

   **{{"aGFoYWhhaGE=" | b64decode}}**

# Security management

The last section in this chapter is about security management. If you tell your sysadmin that you want to introduce a new feature or a tool, one of the first questions they would ask you would be; "what security feature(s) are present with your tool?". We'll try to answer these questions from an Ansible perspective in this section. Let's look at them in greater detail.

## Using Ansible vault

Ansible vault is an exciting feature of Ansible that was introduced in Ansible version 1.5. This allows you to have encrypted passwords as part of your source code. A recommended practice is to NOT have passwords (as well as any other sensitive information such as private keys, SSL certificates, and so on.) in plain text as part of your repository because anyone who checks out your repository can view your passwords. Ansible vault can help you to secure your confidential information by encrypting and decrypting them on your behalf.

Ansible vault supports an interactive mode in which it will ask you for the password, or a non-interactive mode where you will have to specify the file containing the password and Ansible vault will read it directly.

For these examples, we will use the password `ansible`, so let's start creating a hidden file called `.password` with the string `ansible` in it. To do so, let's execute:

   **echo 'ansible' > .password**

We can now create an `ansible-vault` both in the interactive and non-interactive modes. If we want to do it in interactive mode, we will need to execute:

**ansible-vault create secret.yaml**

Ansible will ask us for the vault password and then confirm it. Later it will open the default text editor (in my case **vi**) to add the content in clear. I have used the password `ansible` and the text is This is a password protected file. We can now save and close the editor and check that `ansible-vault` has encrypted our content, in fact if we run:

**cat secret.yaml**

This will output the following:

```
$ANSIBLE_VAULT;1.1;AES256
6634643133393366346138333139376366653837316333653635333564653232313538
36306
46366
3432353561393533362376432396166663932613232333137306336363630326166
6643330393
56565
6464373562616264616631386136653232316164613733336343333363930623034
613436383
33737
6534326135326430390a6437393364616163343138333133363343030666662653
8643531386
66233
3838626638663538363703063033393839623633623333364346432613062363830
3163306
53866
6431343764386132663066363037613465326463363263333432643861
```

In the same way, we can invoke the `ansible-vault` command with the `-vault-password-file=VAULT_PASSWORD_FILE` option to specify our `.password` file. We can, for instance, edit our `secret.yaml` file with the command:

**ansible-vault --vault-password-file=.password edit secret.yaml**

This will open your default text editor where you'll be able to change the file as if it was a plain file. When you save the file, Ansible vault will perform the encryption before saving it, assuring the confidentiality of your content.

Sometimes you need to look at the content of a file but you don't want to open it in a text editor, so you usually use `cat` command. Ansible vault has a similar feature called `view`, so you can run:

**ansible-vault --vault-password-file=.password view secret.yaml**

Ansible vault allows you to decrypt a file, replacing its encrypted content with its plain text content. To do so, you can execute:

```
ansible-vault --vault-password-file=.password decrypt secret.yaml
```

At this point, we can the `cat` command on the `secret.yaml` file and the result is the following:

```
This is a password protected file
```

Ansible vault also gives you the capability to encrypt files that already exist. This is particularly useful if you want to develop all your files on a trusted machine (for instance your own local machine) in a clear text to improve your efficiency and then encrypt all sensible files afterward. To do so, you can execute:

```
ansible-vault --vault-password-file=.password encrypt secret.yaml
```

You can now check that the `secret.yaml` file is now encrypted again.

The last option of the Ansible vault is very important since it's a `rekey` function. This function will allow you to change the encryption key in a single command. You could perform the same operation with two commands (decrypt the `secret.yaml` file with the **old key** and then encrypt it with the **new key**) but being able to perform it in a single step has major advantages since the file in its clear-text form will not be stored on the disk at any moment of the process. To do so we need a file containing the new password (in our case, the file called `.newpassword` and containing the string `ansible2`), and you need to execute the following command:

```
ansible-vault --vault-password-file=.password --new-vault-password-file=.newpassword rekey secret.yaml
```

We can now use the `cat` command on to the `secret.yaml` file and we will see the following output:

```
$ANSIBLE_VAULT;1.1;AES256
633138646434346639933313233353733636231313361643037646361383335336632666230
3832
643131613161303334326637313735616638356432623430a386236633635333939333234643
435
64353932383930613934343730386635333030373663313631646462613566313336323133363
39135
3935613661373263330a3166343335366534613565353836623764646564666623536363537
386462
31636637346538636161616632313866636365666361633138666134303433331666537623732
6162
3638653738383830323430313161336436532326461636343234
```

This is very different from the previous one we had.

## Vaults and playbooks

You can also use vaults with `ansible-playbook`. You'll need to decrypt the file on-the-fly using a command such as the following:

```
$ ansible-playbook site.yml --vault-password-file .password
```

There is yet another option that allows you to decrypt files using a script, which can then look up some other source and decrypt the file. This can also be a useful option to provide more security. However, make sure that the `get_password.py` script has executable permissions:

```
$ ansible-playbook site.yml --vault-password-file ~/.get_password.py
```

Before closing this chapter, I'd like to speak a little bit about the password file. This file needs to be present on the machine where you execute your playbooks, in a location and with permissions so that is readable by the user who is executing the playbook. You can create the `.password` file at startup. The '.' character in the `.password` filename is to make sure that the file is hidden by default when you look for it. This is not directly a security measure, but could help mitigate cases where an attacker does not know exactly what he is looking for.

The `.password` file content should be a password or key that is secure and accessible only to folks who have permission to run Ansible playbooks.

Finally, make sure that you're not encrypting every file that's available! Ansible vault should be used only for important information that needs to be secure.

> Every time you'll save an encrypted file, no matter if changes have been applied or not, the file will be re-encrypted and therefore will change in encrypted content. This will cause your SCM tool to mark the file as modified.

# Encrypting user passwords

Ansible vault takes care of passwords that are checked in and helps you handle them while running Ansible playbooks or commands. However, when Ansible plays are run, at times you might need your users to enter passwords. You also want to make sure that these passwords don't appear in the comprehensive Ansible logs (the default location: /var/log/ansible.log) or on stdout.

Ansible uses Passlib, which is a password hashing library for Python, to handle encryption for prompted passwords. You can use any of the following algorithms supported by Passlib:

- des_crypt: DES Crypt
- bsdi_crypt: BSDi Crypt
- bigcrypt: BigCrypt
- crypt16: Crypt16
- md5_crypt: MD5 Crypt
- bcrypt: BCrypt
- sha1_crypt: SHA-1 Crypt
- sun_md5_crypt: Sun MD5 Crypt
- sha256_crypt: SHA-256 Crypt
- sha512_crypt: SHA-512 Crypt
- apr_md5_crypt: Apache's MD5-Crypt variant
- phpass: PHPass' Portable Hash
- pbkdf2_digest: Generic PBKDF2 Hashes
- cta_pbkdf2_sha1: Cryptacular's PBKDF2 hash
- dlitz_pbkdf2_sha1: Dwayne Litzenberger's PBKDF2 hash
- scram: SCRAM Hash
- bsd_nthash: FreeBSD's MCF-compatible nthash encoding

Let's now see how encryption works with a variable prompt:

```
vars_prompt:
- name: ssh_password
  prompt: Enter ssh_password
  private: True
  encryption: md5_crypt
  confirm: True
  salt_size: 7
```

In the preceding snippet, `vars_prompt` is used to prompt users for some data. The `vars_prompt` is not a task but is another section at the same level as the `tasks:` one.

The `name` module indicates the actual variable name where Ansible will store the user password, as shown in the following command:

**name: ssh_password**

We are using the `prompt` utility to prompt users for the password as follows:

**prompt: Enter ssh password**

We are explicitly asking Ansible to hide the password from `stdout` by using `private` module; this works like any other password prompt on a Unix system. The `private` module is accessed as follows:

**private: True**

We are using the `md5_crypt` algorithm over here with a salt size of 7:

**encrypt: md5_crypt**
**salt_size: 7**

Moreover, Ansible will prompt for the password twice and compare both passwords:

**confirm: True**

## Hiding passwords

Ansible, by default, filters output that contains the `login_password` key, the `password` key, and the `user:pass` format. For example, if you are passing a password in your module using `login_password` or the `password` key, then Ansible will replace your password with `VALUE_HIDDEN`. Let's now see how you can hide a password using the `password` key:

```
- name: Running a script
  shell: script.sh
    password: my_password
```

In the preceding `shell` task, we use the `password` key to pass passwords. This will allow Ansible to hide it from `stdout` and its log file.

*Handling Complex Deployment*

Now, when you run the preceding task in the *verbose* mode, you should not see your `mypass` password; instead Ansible, with `VALUE_HIDDEN`, will replace it as follows:

**REMOTE_MODULE command script.sh password=VALUE_HIDDEN #USE_SHELL**

 Ansible will protect the strings you declared as password even if they are being used in a different context. For instance, if you have another variable that contains the string `my_password`, if you are going to print it, `HIDDEN_VALUE` will appear, even if that specific variable has not been declared as the password.

## Using no_log

Ansible will hide your passwords only if you are using a specific set of keys. However, this might not be the case every time; moreover, you might also want to hide some other confidential data. The `no_log` feature of Ansible will hide your entire task from logging it to the `syslog` file. It will still print your task on `stdout` and log it to other Ansible logfiles.

 At the time of writing this book, Ansible did not support hiding tasks from `stdout` using `no_log`.

Another way to prevent Ansible from logging is to set in the `ansible.cfg` file, in the `[defaults]` section, `log_path` with the value `/dev/null` so that all logs are saved in `/dev/null`, and therefore lost.

Let's now see how you can hide an entire task with `no_log` as follows:

```
- name: Running a script
  shell: script.sh
    password: my_password
  no_log: True
```

By passing `no_log: True` to your task, Ansible will prevent the entire task from hitting syslog.

# Summary

In this chapter, we have seen a very large number of Ansible features. We started with `local_actions` for performing operations on a machine, then we moved to the delegation for performing the task on a third machine. We then moved to conditionals and include for making playbooks more flexible. We learned about roles and how they can help you keep your system aligned and learned how to organize an Ansible repository properly, making the most of Ansible and Git. Later, we covered execution strategies and Jinja filters for more flexible executions.

We ended this chapter with Ansible vault and many other tips to make your Ansible execution safer.

In the next chapter, we will be looking at how to use Ansible to create infrastructures and more specifically, how to do it using the cloud providers, AWS and DigitalOcean.

# 5
# Going Cloud

In this chapter, we will see how to use Ansible for provisioning infrastructures in a matter of minutes. In my opinion, this is one of the most interesting and powerful capabilities of Ansible, since it allows you to (re-)create environments in a quick and consistent way. This is very important when you have multiple environments for the various stages of your deployment pipeline. In fact, it allows you to create equal environments and to keep them aligned when you need to make changes without any pain.

Letting Ansible provision your machines also has other advantages, and for those reasons I always suggest to do:

- **Audit trail**: In the last few years, the IT sector swallowed a huge number of other sectors and as a consequence of this, the auditing processes are now looking at IT as a critical part of the process. When an auditor comes to the IT department asking for the history of a server, from its creation to the present moment, having Ansible playbooks for the whole process helps a lot.
- **Multiple staging environments**: As we mentioned before, if you have multiple environments, provisioning servers with Ansible will help you a lot
- **Moving servers**: When a company uses a global cloud provider (like AWS or DigitalOcean) they often choose the region closest to their offices or customers at the moment they create the first servers. Those providers often open new regions and if their new region is close to you; you may want to move or extend your infrastructure to the new region. This would be a nightmare if you had provisioned every resource manually.

In this chapter, at a broad level, we'll cover the following topics:

- Provisioning of machines in **Amazon Web Services** (**AWS**)
- Provisioning of machines in DigitalOcean
- Provisioning Docker containers

Most of the new machine creations have two phases:

- Provisioning a new machine or a new set of machines
- Running playbooks to ensure the new machines are configured properly to play their role in your infrastructure

We've looked at the configuration management aspect in the initial chapters. We'll focus a lot more on provisioning new machines in this chapter with a lesser focus on configuration management.

## Provisioning resources in the cloud

With that, let's jump to the first topic. Teams managing infrastructures have a lot of choices today for running their builds, tests, and deployments. Providers such as Amazon, Rackspace, and DigitalOcean primarily provide **Infrastructure as a Service** (**IaaS**). When we speak about IaaS, it's better to speak about resources not virtual machines for different reasons:

- The majority of the products that those companies allow you to provision are not machines but other critical resources such as networking and storage
- Lately, many of those companies have started to provide many different kind of compute instances ranging from bare-metal machines to containers
- Setting up machines with no networking (or storage) could be all you need for some very simple environments, but might not be enough in production environments

Those companies usually provide API, CLI, GUI, and SDK utilities to create and manage cloud resources throughout their whole lifecycle. We're more interested in using their SDK as it will play an important part in our automation effort. Setting up new servers and provisioning them is interesting at first but at some stage it can become boring as it's quite repetitive in nature. Each provisioning step will involve several similar steps to get them up-and-running.

Imagine one fine morning you receive an e-mail asking for three new customer setups, where each customer setup has three to four instances and a bunch of services and dependencies. This might be an easy task for you, but would require running the same set of repetitive commands multiple times, followed by monitoring the servers once they come up to confirm that everything went well. In addition, anything you do manually has a chance of introducing problems. What if two of the customer setups come up correctly but, due to fatigue, you miss out a step for the third customer and hence introduce a problem?

To deal with such situations, there exists automation.

Cloud provisioning automation makes it easy for an engineer to build up a new server as quickly as possible, allowing her to concentrate on other priorities. Using Ansible, you can easily perform these actions and automate cloud provisioning with minimal effort. Ansible provides you with the power to automate various different cloud platforms, such as Amazon, Azure, DigitalOcean, Google Cloud, Rackspace, and many more, with modules for different services available in the Ansible core or extended module packages.

 As mentioned earlier, bringing up new machines is not the end of the game. We also need to make sure we configure them to play the required role.

In the next sections we will provision the environment that we have used in the previous chapters (two web servers and one database server) in the following environments:

- **Simple Amazon Web Service deployment**: Where all machines will be placed in the same Availability Zone and same network
- **Complex Amazon Web Service deployment**: Where the machines will be split in multiple Availability Zones as well as networks
- **DigitalOcean**: DigitalOcean does not allow us to do many networking tweaks so it will be similar to the first one
- **Docker**: We will create a simple deployment in this case

## Amazon Web Service

Amazon Web Service is the most used public cloud by a fair amount and it's often chosen due to their huge amount of available services as well as the huge amount of documentation, answered questions, and articles that can be expected from such a popular product.

Since AWS' goal is to be a complete virtual data center provider (and much more) we will need to create and manage our network as we would do if we had to set up a real data center. Obviously, we will not need to cable stuff since it's a virtual data center. Due to this, a few lines of an Ansible playbook will be enough.

# AWS global infrastructure

Amazon has always been pretty discrete about sharing the location or the exact number of data centers that their cloud is actually composed of. While I'm writing this, AWS counts 13 regions (with 4 more regions already planned) with a total of 35 **Availability Zones** (**AZ**) and more than 50 edge locations. Amazon defines a region as a physical location in the world where we (Amazon) have multiple Availability Zones. Looking at Amazon's definition of Availability Zones, it says that an AZ consists of one or more discrete data centers, each with redundant power, networking, and connectivity, housed in separate facilities. For edge location, there is no official definition.

As you can see, from a real life point of view, those definitions do not help you much. When I try to explain those concepts I usually use different definitions, created by myself:

- **Region**: Group of AZs that are physically close
- **Availability Zone**: A data center in a region (Amazon says that it could be more than one data center, but since there is no document listing the specific layout of every AZ, I assume the worst-case scenario)
- **Edge location**: Internet exchanges or 3rd party data centers where Amazon has S3 and Route 53 endpoints

Even though I tried to make those definitions as easy and as useful as possible, some of them are very cloudy. When we start to speak about real world differences, the definitions will become immediately clear. For instance, from a network speed perspective, when you move content within the same AZ, the bandwidth is very high. When you do the same operation with two AZs in the same region you get high bandwidth, while if you use two AZs from two different regions, the bandwidth will be much lower. Also, there is a price difference, since all traffic within the same region is free, while traffic between different regions is not free of charge.

# AWS Simple Storage Service

Amazon S3 is the first AWS service to be launched and it's also one of the most well-known AWS services. Amazon S3 is an object storage service with public endpoints as well as private endpoints. It uses the concept of a bucket to allow you different kinds of files and to manage them in a simple way. Amazon S3 also gives the user more advanced features such as the capability of serving a bucket's contents using a built-in web server. This is one of the reasons why many people decide to host their website, or the pictures on their websites, on Amazon S3.

The advantages of S3 are mainly:

- **Price schema**: You are billed by used gigabyte/month and by gigabyte transferred.
- **Reliability**: Amazon affirms that the objects on AWS S3 have a 99.999999999% probability to survive any given year. This is orders of magnitude higher than any hard disk.
- **Tooling**: Since S3 is a service that has been out there for many years now, a lot of tools have been implemented to leverage this service.

# AWS Elastic Compute Cloud (EC2)

The second service launched by AWS is the EC2 service. This service allows you to spin up virtual machines on AWS infrastructure. You can think of those EC2 instances as OpenStack compute instances or VMware virtual machines. Initially, those machines were very similar to VPS, but after a while, Amazon decided to give much more flexibility on those machines introducing a very advanced networking option. The old kind of machines are still available in the oldest data centers with the name **EC2 Classic**, while the new kind is the current default and is just called **EC2**.

# AWS Virtual Private Cloud (VPC)

The VPC is Amazon's networking implementation which we mentioned in the previous paragraph. The VPC is more a set of tools than a single tool, in fact, the capabilities it offers were offered by multiple metal boxes in the classic data center. The main things you can create with VPC are:

- Switches
- Routers
- DHCP
- Gateways
- Firewalls
- Virtual Private Networks

Going Cloud

An important thing to understand when you use VPC is that the layout of your network is not completely arbitrary, since Amazon has created a few limitations to simplify their networking. The basic limitations are:

- You cannot spawn a subnetwork between AZ
- You cannot spawn a network between regions
- You cannot route networks in different regions directly

While, for the first two, the only solution is creating multiple networks and subnetworks, for the third, you can actually implement a workaround using a VPN service which could be self-provisioned or be provisioned using the official AWS VPN service.

We will be mainly using the switching and routing capabilities of VPC.

## AWS Route 53

Like many other cloud services, Amazon offers a **DNS as a Service** (**DNSaaS**) feature and in Amazon case, it's called **Route 53**. Route 53 is a distributed DNS service with more than 50 endpoints worldwide (Route 53 is present in all AWS edge locations).

Route 53 allows you to create different zones for a domain allowing split-horizon situations in which, based on the fact that the client asking for a DNS resolution is inside or outside your VPC, will receive different responses. This is very useful when you want your applications to be easily moved in and out of your VPC without changes but at the same time, you want your traffic to stay on a private (virtual) network whenever possible.

## AWS Elastic Block Storage (EBS)

AWS **EBS** is a block storage provider for allowing your EC2 instances to keep data that will survive reboots and is very flexible. From a user perspective, EBS seems a lot like any other SAN product with a simpler interface, since you only need to create the volume and tell EBS to which machine it needs to be attached, and EBS does the rest. You can attach multiple volumes to a single server, but every volume can be connected to only one server at any given time.

## AWS Identity and Access Management

To allow you to manage users and access methods, Amazon provides the **IAM** service. The main features of the IAM service are:

- Create, edit, and delete users
- Change user password
- Create, edit, and delete groups
- Manage users and group association
- Manage tokens
- Manage two-factor authentication
- Manage SSH keys

We will be using this service to set up our users and their permissions.

## Amazon relational database service

Setting up and maintaining relational databases is complex and very time-consuming. To simplify this, Amazon provides some widely used DBaaS, more specifically:

- Aurora
- MariaDB
- MySQL
- Oracle
- PostgreSQL
- SQL Server

For each one of those engines, Amazon offers different features and price models but the specifics of each is beyond the goal of this book.

## Setting up an account with AWS

The first thing we will need before starting to work on our Amazon Web Service is an account. Creating an account on Amazon Web Services is pretty straightforward and very well-documented by Amazon official documentation as well as by multiple independent sites and therefore it will not be covered in these pages.

After you have created your AWS account, you need to go into the AWS and do the following:

- Upload your SSH key in **EC2** | **Keypairs**
- Create a new user in **Identity & Access Management** | **Users** | **Create new user** and create a file in ~/.aws/credentials with the following lines:

```
[default]
aws_access_key_id = YOUR_ACCESS_KEY
aws_secret_access_key = YOUR_SECRET_KEY
```

After you have created your AWS Keys and uploaded your SSH key, you need to set up Route53. In Route53 you need to create two zones for your domain (you can also use a subdomain if you don't have an unused domain): one **public** and one **private**.

If you create only the public zone, Route53 will propagate this zone everywhere, but if you create a public and a private zone, Route53 will serve your public zone everywhere but in the VPC you specified when creating the private zone. If you query those DNS entries from within that VPC, the private zone will be used. This approach has multiple advantages:

- Only publicize the IP addresses of public machines
- Always use DNS names instead of IP addresses, even for internal traffic
- Ensure that your internal machines communicate directly without your traffic ever passing through the public web
- Since the external IPs in Amazon Web Services are virtual IPs managed by Amazon and associated to your instances using NATs, this approach grants the least amount of hops and therefore latency

If you declared an entry for your public zone but not in the private one, the machines in the VPC will not be able to resolve that entry.

After you have created the public zone, Amazon Web Services will give you a few name server IP addresses and you need to put those in your register/root zone DNS so that you can actually resolve those DNS.

# Simple AWS deployment

As we said previously, the first thing that we will need is the networking up. For this example, we will need just one single network in one AZ and all our machines will stay there.

In this section, we will be working in the `playbooks/aws_simple_provision.yaml` file.

The first two lines are just used to declare the host that will perform the commands (`localhost`) and the beginning of the `tasks` section:

```
- hosts: localhost
  tasks:
```

In AWS, we need to have a VPC network and subnetwork, but in case you need it, you can do the following to create the VPC network:

```
To create the VPC subnetwork:
  - name: Ensure the VPC subnetwork is present
    ec2_vpc_subnet:
      state: present
      az: AWS_AZ
      vpc_id: '{{ aws_simple_net.vpc_id }}'
      cidr: 10.0.1.0/24
    register: aws_subnet
```

Now we have all the information we need on the network and subnetwork, we can move to **security groups**. We can do this with the `ec2_group` module. In the Amazon Web Service world, security groups are used for firewalling. Security groups are very similar to groups of firewall rules that share the same destination (for ingress rules) or same destination (for egress rules). Three differences with standard firewalls rules are actually worth mentioning:

- Multiple security groups can be applied to the same EC2 instance
- As source (for ingress rules) or destination (for egress rules), you can specify one of the following:
  - An instance ID
  - Another security group
  - An IP range
- You don't have to specify a default deny rule at the end of the chain because AWS will add it by default

```
- name: Ensure websg Security Group is present
  ec2_group:
```

```
          name: web
          description: Web Security Group
          region: AWS_AZ
          vpc_id: VPC_ID
          rules:
          - proto: tcp
            from_port: 80
            to_port: 80
            cidr_ip: 0.0.0.0/0
          - proto: tcp
            from_port: 443
            to_port: 443
            cidr_ip: 0.0.0.0/0
          rules_egress:
          - proto: all
            cidr_ip: 0.0.0.0/0
          register: aws_simple_websg
```

So, in my case, the following code will be added to playbooks/aws_simple_provision.yaml:

```
        - name: Ensure wssg Security Group is present
          ec2_group:
            name: wssg
            description: Web Security Group
            region: eu-west-1
            vpc_id: '{{ aws_simple_net.vpcs.0.id }}'
            rules:
            - proto: tcp
              from_port: 22
              to_port: 22
              cidr_ip: 0.0.0.0/0
            - proto: tcp
              from_port: 80
              to_port: 80
              cidr_ip: 0.0.0.0/0
            - proto: tcp
              from_port: 443
              to_port: 443
              cidr_ip: 0.0.0.0/0
            rules_egress:
            - proto: all
              cidr_ip: 0.0.0.0/0
          register: aws_simple_wssg
```

Chapter 5

We are now going to create another security group for our database. In this case, we only need to open port 3036 to the servers in the web security group:

```
- name: Ensure dbsg Security Group is present
  ec2_group:
    name: dbsg
    description: DB Security Group
    region: eu-west-1
    vpc_id: '{{ aws_simple_net.vpcs.0.id }}'
    rules:
    - proto: tcp
      from_port: 3036
      to_port: 3036
      group_id: '{{ aws_simple_wssg.group_id }}'
    rules_egress:
    - proto: all
      cidr_ip: 0.0.0.0/0
  register: aws_simple_dbsg
```

As you can see, we allow all egress traffic to flow. This is not what security best practices suggest, and therefore you may need to regulate egress traffic as well. A case that frequently forces you to regulate egress traffic is if you want your target machine to be PCI-DSS compliant.

Now that we have the VPC, the subnet into the VPC, and the needed security groups, we can now move on to actually creating the EC2 instances:

```
- name: Setup instances
  ec2:
    assign_public_ip: '{{ item.assign_public_ip }}'
    image: ami-7abd0209
    region: eu-west-1
    exact_count: 1
    key_name: fale
    count_tag:
      Name: '{{ item.name }}'
    instance_tags:
      Name: '{{ item.name }}'
    instance_type: t2.micro
    group_id: '{{ item.group_id }}'
    vpc_subnet_id: '{{ aws_simple_subnet.subnets.0.id }}'
    volumes:
      - device_name: /dev/sda1
        volume_type: gp2
        volume_size: 10
        delete_on_termination: True
  register: aws_simple_instances
```

[ 129 ]

```
with_items:
  - name: ws01.simple.aws.fale.io
    group_id: '{{ aws_simple_wssg.group_id }}'
    assign_public_ip: True
  - name: ws02.simple.aws.fale.io
    group_id: '{{ aws_simple_wssg.group_id }}'
    assign_public_ip: True
  - name: db01.simple.aws.fale.io
    group_id: '{{ aws_simple_dbsg.group_id }}'
    assign_public_ip: False
```

 When we created the `db` machine we did not specify the `assign_public_ip: True` line. In this case, the machine will not receive a public IP and therefore it will not be reachable from outside our VPC. Since we used a very strict security group for this server, it would not be reachable from any machine outside the `wssg` anyway.

As you can guess, the piece of code we have just seen will create our three instances (two web servers and one database server).

We can now proceed to add those newly created instances to our Route 53 account so that we can resolve those machines' FQDN. To interact with AWS Route 53, we will be using the `route53` module, which allows us to create entries, query entries, and delete entries. To create a new entry, we will be using the following code:

```
- name: Add route53 entry for server SERVER_NAME
  route53:
    command: create
    zone: ZONE_NAME
    record: RECORD_TO_ADD
    type: RECORD_TYPE
    ttl: TIME_TO_LIVE
    value: IP_VALUES
    wait: True
```

So to create the entries for our servers, we will add the following code:

```
- name: Add route53 rules for instances
  route53:
    command: create
    zone: aws.fale.io
    record: '{{ item.tagged_instances.0.tags.Name }}'
    type: A
    ttl: 1
    value: '{{ item.tagged_instances.0.public_ip }}'
    wait: True
  with_items: '{{ aws_simple_instances.results }}'
```

```yaml
      when: item.tagged_instances.0.public_ip
    - name: Add internal route53 rules for instances
      route53:
        command: create
        zone: aws.fale.io
        private_zone: True
        record: '{{ item.tagged_instances.0.tags.Name }}'
        type: A
        ttl: 1
        value: '{{ item.tagged_instances.0.private_ip }}'
        wait: True
      with_items: '{{ aws_simple_instances.results }}'
```

Since the database server does not have a public address, it makes no sense to publish this machine in the public zone, so we have created this machine entry only in the internal zone.

Putting it all together, the `playbooks/aws_simple_provision.yaml` will be the following:

```yaml
- hosts: localhost
  tasks:
  - name: Gather information of the EC2 VPC net in eu-west-1
    ec2_vpc_net_facts:
      region: eu-west-1
    register: aws_simple_net
  - name: Gather information of the EC2 VPC subnet in eu-west-1
    ec2_vpc_subnet_facts:
      region: eu-west-1
      filters:
        vpc-id: '{{ aws_simple_net.vpcs.0.id }}'
    register: aws_simple_subnet
  - name: Ensure wssg Security Group is present
    ec2_group:
      name: wssg
      description: Web Security Group
      region: eu-west-1
      vpc_id: '{{ aws_simple_net.vpcs.0.id }}'
      rules:
      - proto: tcp
        from_port: 22
        to_port: 22
        cidr_ip: 0.0.0.0/0
      - proto: tcp
        from_port: 80
        to_port: 80
```

```yaml
              cidr_ip: 0.0.0.0/0
            - proto: tcp
              from_port: 443
              to_port: 443
              cidr_ip: 0.0.0.0/0
            rules_egress:
            - proto: all
              cidr_ip: 0.0.0.0/0
          register: aws_simple_wssg
        - name: Ensure dbsg Security Group is present
          ec2_group:
            name: dbsg
            description: DB Security Group
            region: eu-west-1
            vpc_id: '{{ aws_simple_net.vpcs.0.id }}'
            rules:
            - proto: tcp
              from_port: 3036
              to_port: 3036
              group_id: '{{ aws_simple_wssg.group_id }}'
            rules_egress:
            - proto: all
              cidr_ip: 0.0.0.0/0
          register: aws_simple_dbsg
        - name: Setup instances
          ec2:
            assign_public_ip: '{{ item.assign_public_ip }}'
            image: ami-7abd0209
            region: eu-west-1
            exact_count: 1
            key_name: fale
            count_tag:
              Name: '{{ item.name }}'
            instance_tags:
              Name: '{{ item.name }}'
            instance_type: t2.micro
            group_id: '{{ item.group_id }}'
            vpc_subnet_id: '{{ aws_simple_subnet.subnets.0.id }}'
            volumes:
              - device_name: /dev/sda1
                volume_type: gp2
                volume_size: 10
                delete_on_termination: True
          register: aws_simple_instances
          with_items:
          - name: ws01.simple.aws.fale.io
            group_id: '{{ aws_simple_wssg.group_id }}'
            assign_public_ip: True
```

```yaml
      - name: ws02.simple.aws.fale.io
        group_id: '{{ aws_simple_wssg.group_id }}'
        assign_public_ip: True
      - name: db01.simple.aws.fale.io
        group_id: '{{ aws_simple_dbsg.group_id }}'
        assign_public_ip: False
  - name: Add route53 rules for instances
    route53:
      command: create
      zone: aws.fale.io
      record: '{{ item.tagged_instances.0.tags.Name }}'
      type: A
      ttl: 1
      value: '{{ item.tagged_instances.0.public_ip }}'
      wait: True
    with_items: '{{ aws_simple_instances.results }}'
    when: item.tagged_instances.0.public_ip
  - name: Add internal route53 rules for instances
    route53:
      command: create
      zone: aws.fale.io
      private_zone: True
      record: '{{ item.tagged_instances.0.tags.Name }}'
      type: A
      ttl: 1
      value: '{{ item.tagged_instances.0.private_ip }}'
      wait: True
    with_items: '{{ aws_simple_instances.results }}'
```

Running it with `ansible-playbook playbooks/aws_simple_provision.yaml`, we will have an output similar to:

```
PLAY [localhost] *************************************************
TASK [setup] *****************************************************
ok: [localhost]

TASK [Gather information of the EC2 VPC net in eu-west-1] **********
ok: [localhost]

TASK [Gather information of the EC2 VPC subnet in eu-west-1] *******
ok: [localhost]

TASK [Ensure wssg Security Group is present] **********************
changed: [localhost]

TASK [Ensure dbsg Security Group is present] **********************
changed: [localhost]
```

```
TASK [Setup instances] *******************************************
changed: [localhost] => (item={u'group_id': u'sg-950c2cf2', u'name':
u'ws01.simple.aws.fale.io', u'assign_public_ip': True})
changed: [localhost] => (item={u'group_id': u'sg-950c2cf2', u'name':
u'ws02.simple.aws.fale.io', u'assign_public_ip': True})
changed: [localhost] => (item={u'group_id': u'sg-940c2cf3', u'name':
u'db01.simple.aws.fale.io', u'assign_public_ip': False})

TASK [Add route53 rules for instances] ****************************
changed: [localhost] =>
....

changed: [localhost] =>
....

skipping: [localhost] =>
....

TASK [Add internal route53 rules for instances] ******************
changed: [localhost] =>
....

changed: [localhost] =>
....

changed: [localhost] =>
....

PLAY RECAP *******************************************************
localhost                  : ok=7    changed=4    unreachable=0    failed=0
```

# Complex AWS deployment

In this paragraph, we will slightly change the previous example to move one of the web servers to another AZ within the same region. To do so, we are going to make a new file in `playbooks/aws_complex_provision.yaml` which will be very similar to the previous one, with one difference located in the part that helps us provision the machines. In fact, we will use the following code instead of the one we used on the previous run:

```
- name: Setup instances
  ec2:
    assign_public_ip: '{{ item.assign_public_ip }}'
    image: ami-7abd0209
    region: eu-west-1
    exact_count: 1
```

```yaml
      key_name: fale
      count_tag:
        Name: '{{ item.name }}'
      instance_tags:
        Name: '{{ item.name }}'
      instance_type: t2.micro
      group_id: '{{ item.group_id }}'
      vpc_subnet_id: '{{ item.vpc_subnet_id }}'
      volumes:
        - device_name: /dev/sda1
          volume_type: gp2
          volume_size: 10
          delete_on_termination: True
  register: aws_simple_instances
  with_items:
  - name: ws01.simple.aws.fale.io
    group_id: '{{ aws_simple_wssg.group_id }}'
    assign_public_ip: True
    vpc_subnet_id: '{{ aws_simple_subnet.subnets.0.id }}'
  - name: ws02.simple.aws.fale.io
    group_id: '{{ aws_simple_wssg.group_id }}'
    assign_public_ip: True
    vpc_subnet_id: '{{ aws_simple_subnet.subnets.1.id }}'
  - name: db01.simple.aws.fale.io
    group_id: '{{ aws_simple_dbsg.group_id }}'
    assign_public_ip: False
    vpc_subnet_id: '{{ aws_simple_subnet.subnets.0.id }}'
```

As you can see, we have put the `vpc_subnet_id` in a variable, so that we can use a different one for the `ws02` machine. Due to the fact that AWS already provides two subnets by default (and every subnet is tied to a different AZ), it's enough to use the following AZ. Security groups and Route 53 code does not need to be changed since it does not work at a subnet/AZ level, but at a VPC level (for security groups and internal Route 53 zone) or global level (for public Route 53).

# DigitalOcean

Compared to Amazon Web Services, DigitalOcean seems to be very incomplete. DigitalOcean, until a few months ago only provided droplets, SSH key management, and DNS management. At the time of writing this, DigitalOcean has very recently launched an additional block storage service. The advantages of DigitalOcean compared to many competitors are:

- Lower prices than AWS

- Very easy APIs
- Very well documented APIs
- The droplets are very similar to standard virtual machines (they don't do weird customization)
- The droplets are very quick to go up and down
- Since DigitalOcean has a very simple networking stack, it's way more efficient than the AWS one

# Droplets

Droplets are the main service offered by DigitalOcean and are compute instances which are very similar to Amazon EC2 classic. DigitalOcean relies on the **Kernel Virtual Machine** (**KVM**) to virtualize the machines, assuring very high performance and security. Since they do not change KVM in any sensible way, and since KVM is open source and available on any Linux machine, this allows system administrators to create identical environments on private and public clouds. DigitalOcean droplets will have one external IP and they can be eventually added to a virtual network that will allow your machines to use internal IPs.

Different from many other comparable services, DigitalOcean allows your droplets to have IPv6 IPs in addition to the IPv4 ones. This service is free of charge.

# SSH key management

Every time you want to create a droplet, you have to specify if you want a specific SSH key assigned to the `root` user or if you want a password (which will have to be changed at the first login). To be able to choose an SSH key, you need an interface to upload it. DigitalOcean allows you to do this using a very simple interface which allows you to list the current keys, as well as create and delete keys.

## Private networking

As mentioned in the droplet paragraph, DigitalOcean allows us to have a private network where our machine can communicate with another. This allows segregation of services (like a database service) only on the internal network to allow a higher level of security. Since by default, MySQL binds on all available interfaces, we will need to tweak the database role a little bit to only bind on the internal network.

To recognize the internal network from the external one there are many ways, due to some DigitalOcean peculiarities:

- Private networks are always in the `10.0.0.0/8` network, while public IPs are never in that network
- The public network is always `eth0` while the private network is always `eth1`

Based on your portability needs, you can use either one of those strategies to understand where to bind your services.

## Adding an SSH key in DigitalOcean

You need to have a DigitalOcean user with the credit card set up, and have obtained API key. To perform those operations, you can use DigitalOcean web interface. We can now start to use Ansible to add our SSH key to our DigitalOcean cloud. To do so, we need to create a file called `playbooks/do_provision.yaml` with the following structure:

```
- hosts: localhost
  tasks:
  - name: Add the SSH Key to Digital Ocean
    digital_ocean:
      state: present
      command: ssh
      name: SSH_KEY_NAME
      ssh_pub_key: 'ssh-rsa AAAA...'
      api_token: XXX
    register: ssh_key
```

In my case, this is my file content:

```
- hosts: localhost
  tasks:
  - name: Add the SSH Key to Digital Ocean
    digital_ocean:
      state: present
      command: ssh
```

```
            name: faleKey
            ssh_pub_key: 'ssh-rsa AAAA...=='
            api_token: 259...b3b
        register: ssh_key
```

Then we can execute it with:

```
ansible-playbook -i localhost, playbooks/do_provision.yaml
```

and you will have a result similar to the following:

```
PLAY [localhost] *********************************************
TASK [setup] *************************************************
ok: [localhost]

TASK [Add the SSH Key to Digital Ocean] **********************
changed: [localhost]

PLAY RECAP ***************************************************
localhost                  : ok=2    changed=1    unreachable=0    failed=0
```

This task is idempotent so we can execute it multiple times. In case the key has already been uploaded, the SSH key ID will be returned at every run.

## Deployment in DigitalOcean

At the time of writing, the only way to create a droplet in Ansible is by using the `digital_ocean` module which could be soon deprecated since many of its features are now done in a better, cleaner way by other modules and there is already a bug on Ansible bug tracker to track its complete rewrite and possible deprecation. My guess is that the new module will be called `digital_ocean_droplet` and will have a similar syntax, but at the moment there is no code so it's just my guess.

To create the droplets, we will have to use the `digital_ocean` module with a syntax similar to the following:

```
    - name: Ensure the ws and db servers are present
      digital_ocean:
        state: present
        ssh_key_ids: KEY_ID
        name: '{{ item }}'
        api_token: DIGITAL_OCEAN_KEY
        size_id: 512mb
        region_id: lon1
```

```
      image_id: centos-7-0-x64
      unique_name: True
    with_items:
    - WEBSERVER 1
    - WEBSERVER 2
    - DBSERVER 1
```

To make sure that all our provisioning is done completely and in a sane way, I always suggest creating one single provision file for the whole infrastructure. So, in my case, I'll add the following task to the `playbooks/do_provision.yaml` file:

```
    - name: Ensure the ws and db servers are present
      digital_ocean:
        state: present
        ssh_key_ids: '{{ ssh_key.ssh_key.id }}'
        name: '{{ item }}'
        api_token: 259...b3b
        size_id: 512mb
        region_id: lon1
        image_id: centos-7-0-x64
        unique_name: True
      with_items:
      - ws01.do.fale.io
      - ws02.do.fale.io
      - db01.do.fale.io
      register: droplets
```

After this, we can add the domain with the `digital_ocean_domain` module:

```
    - name: Ensure domain resolve properly
      digital_ocean_domain:
        api_token: 259...b3b
        state: present
        name: '{{ item.droplet.name }}'
        ip: '{{ item.droplet.ip_address }}'
      with_items: '{{ droplets.results }}'
```

So, putting all this together, our `playbooks/do_provision.yaml` will look like this:

```
    - hosts: localhost
      tasks:
      - name: Add the SSH Key to Digital Ocean
        digital_ocean:
          state: present
          command: ssh
          name: faleKey
          ssh_pub_key: 'ssh-rsa AAAA...=='
          api_token: 7e7...f6f
```

```yaml
        register: ssh_key
      - name: Ensure the ws and db servers are present
        digital_ocean:
          state: present
          ssh_key_ids: '{{ ssh_key.ssh_key.id }}'
          name: '{{ item }}'
          api_token: 259...b3b
          size_id: 512mb
          region_id: lon1
          image_id: centos-7-0-x64
          unique_name: True
        with_items:
        - ws01.do.fale.io
        - ws02.do.fale.io
        - db01.do.fale.io
        register: droplets
      - name: Ensure domain resolve properly
        digital_ocean_domain:
          api_token: 259...b3b
          state: present
          name: '{{ item.droplet.name }}'
          ip: '{{ item.droplet.ip_address }}'
        with_items: '{{ droplets.results }}'
```

So we can now run it with the following command:

```
ansible-playbook -i localhost, playbooks/do_provision.yaml
```

We will see a result similar to the following:

```
PLAY [localhost] ******************************************************
TASK [setup] **********************************************************
ok: [localhost]

TASK [Add the SSH Key to Digital Ocean] *******************************
changed: [localhost]

TASK [Ensure the ws and db servers are present] ***********************
changed: [localhost] => (item=ws01.do.fale.io)
changed: [localhost] => (item=ws02.do.fale.io)
changed: [localhost] => (item=db01.do.fale.io)

TASK [Ensure domain resolve properly] *********************************
changed: [localhost] =>
....

changed: [localhost] =>
....
```

```
    changed: [localhost] =>
    ....

    PLAY RECAP **********************************************************
        localhost                  : ok=4    changed=3    unreachable=0    failed=0
```

# Summary

In this chapter, we have seen how we can provision our machines in both the AWS cloud and the DigitalOcean one. In the case of the AWS cloud, we have seen two different examples, one very simple and one slightly more complex.

In the next chapter, we will talk about getting notified by Ansible if something went wrong.

# 6
# Getting Notifications from Ansible

One of the big advantages of Ansible compared to a bash script is its capability of running multiple times on the same system, ensuring that everything is in order. This is a very nice feature that not only assures you that nothing has changed the configurations on your server, but also those new configurations will be applied in a short time.

Due to these reasons, many people run their `master.yaml` once a day. When you do this (and probably you should!), you want some kind of feedback sent to you by Ansible itself. There are also many other cases where you may want Ansible to send messages to you or your team. For instance, if you use Ansible to deploy your application, you may want to send an IRC message (or other kinds of group chat messages) to your development team channel, so that they are all informed of the status of your system.

Other times, you want Ansible to notify Nagios that it's going to break something so that Nagios does not worry and does not start to shoot e-mails and messages to your sysadmins.

In this chapter we'll explore the following topics:

- Mail notifications
- Ansible XMPP/Jabber
- Slack and Rocket Chat
- Sending a message to an IRC channel (community information and contributing)
- Amazon Simple Notification Service
- Nagios

# E-mails

The easiest and most common way of alerting people is to send e-mails. Ansible allows you to send e-mails from your playbook using a `mail` module. You can use this module in between any of your tasks and notify your user whenever required. Also, in some cases, you cannot automate each and every thing because either you lack the authority or it requires some manual checking and confirmation. If this is the case, you can notify the responsible user that Ansible has done its job and it's time for him/her to perform his/her duty. Let's see how you can use the `mail` module to notify your users with a very simple playbook called `uptime_and_email.yaml`:

```yaml
- hosts: localhost
  tasks:
  - name: Read the machine uptime
    command: uptime -p
    register: uptime
  - name: Send the uptime via e-mail
    mail:
       host: mail.fale.io
       username: ansible@fale.io
       password: PASSWORD
       to: me@fale.io
       subject: Ansible-report
       body: 'Local system uptime is {{ uptime.stdout }}.'
```

In the preceding playbook, we will first read the current machine uptime and then send it via e-mail to someone. This example is very easy and will allow us to keep the examples short, but obviously you can generate the e-mails in a similar way in very long and complex playbooks. If we focus on the `mail` task a little bit, we can see that we are using it with the following data:

- An e-mail server to be used to send the e-mail (also with login information, which is required for this server)
- The receiver e-mail address
- The e-mail subject
- The e-mail body

Other interesting parameters that the `mail` module supports are:

- The `attach` parameter: This is used to add attachments to the e-mail that will be generated. This is very useful when, for instance, you want to send a log via an e-mail.
- The `port` parameter: This is used to specify which port is used by the e-mail server.

An interesting thing about this module is that the only mandatory field is `subject`, and not the body, as many people would expect.

We can now proceed to execute the script to validate its functionality with the following:

```
ansible-playbook -i localhost, uptime_and_email.yaml
```

We will have a result similar to the following:

```
PLAY [localhost] *********************************************
TASK [setup] *************************************************
ok: [localhost]

TASK [Read the machine uptime] *******************************
changed: [localhost]

TASK [Send the uptime via e-mail] ****************************
changed: [localhost]

PLAY RECAP ***************************************************
localhost         : ok=3    changed=2    unreachable=0    failed=0
```

Also, as expected, Ansible has sent me an e-mail with the following content:

```
Local system uptime is up 38 min.
```

This module can be used in many different ways. An example of a real world case that I've seen is a playbook that was created to automate a piece of a very long procedure done by multiple people. The procedure, historically, changed owners using the e-mails and every person involved in the procedure was supposed to do their part after an e-mail was received from the owner of the previous piece. They then sent an e-mail at the end of their piece to the next owner. When we started to automate that procedure, we did it for one specific piece and no one noticed that that part was automated. This is not the best way to handle procedures, but it's widely used in organizations and often you cannot change it.

# XMPP

E-mails are slow, unreliable, and often people do not react to them immediately. There are cases where you want to send a real-time message to one of your users. Many organizations rely on XMPP/Jabber for their internal chat system and the great thing is that Ansible is able to directly send messages to XMPP/Jabber users and conference rooms.

Let's tweak the previous example to send uptime information to a user in the file `uptime_and_xmpp_user.yaml`:

```yaml
- hosts: localhost
  tasks:
  - name: Read the machine uptime
    command: 'uptime -p'
    register: uptime
  - name: Send the uptime to user
    jabber:
      user: ansible@fale.io
      password: PASSWORD
      to: me@fale.io
      msg: 'Local system uptime is {{ uptime.stdout }}.'
```

If you want to use the Ansible `jabber` task, you will need to have the library `xmpppy` installed on the system that will perform the task.

As you can see, the `jabber` module is very similar to the `mail` module and requires similar parameters. In the XMPP case, we don't need to specify the server host and port, since that information is automatically gathered by XMPP from the DNS. In cases where we would need to use a different server host or port, we can use respectively, the `host` and `port` parameters.

We can now proceed to execute the script to validate its functionality with the following:

```
ansible-playbook -i localhost, uptime_and_xmpp_user.yaml
```

We will have a result similar to the following:

```
PLAY [localhost] *************************************************
TASK [setup] *****************************************************
ok: [localhost]

TASK [Read the machine uptime] ***********************************
changed: [localhost]
```

```
TASK [Send the uptime to user] **********************************
changed: [localhost]

PLAY RECAP *******************************************************
localhost              : ok=3    changed=2    unreachable=0    failed=0
```

In cases where we want to send a message to a conference room instead of a single user, it is enough to just change the to parameter, adding the appropriate one, that is:

```
to=sysop@conference.fale.io
(mailto:sysop@conference.fale.io)/ansiblebot
```

# Slack

In the last few years, many new chat and collaboration platforms have appeared. One of the most used ones is Slack. Slack is a cloud-based team collaboration tool, and this allows even easier integration with Ansible.

Let's put the following lines in the file uptime_and_slack.yaml:

```
- hosts: localhost
  tasks:
  - name: Read the machine uptime
    command: 'uptime -p'
    register: uptime
  - name: Send the uptime to slack channel
    slack:
      token: TOKEN
      channel: '#ansible'
      msg: 'Local system uptime is {{ uptime.stdout }}.'
```

As we discussed, this module has an even simpler syntax than the XMPP one, in fact it only needs to know the token (which you can generate on the Slack website), the channel to send the message to, and the message itself.

> Since version 1.8 of Ansible, the new version of the Slack token is required, for instance: G522SJP14/D563DW213/7Qws484asdWD4w12Md3avf4FeD.

Run the playbook with the following:

```
ansible-playbook -i localhost, uptime_and_slack.yaml
```

This results in the following output:

```
PLAY [localhost] *********************************************
TASK [setup] *************************************************
ok: [localhost]

TASK [Read the machine uptime] *******************************
changed: [localhost]

TASK [Send the uptime to slack channel] **********************
changed: [localhost]

PLAY RECAP ***************************************************
localhost        : ok=3    changed=2    unreachable=0    failed=0
```

Since Slack's goal is to make communications more efficient, it allows us to tweak multiple aspects of the message. The most interesting points from my point of view are the following:

- `color`: This allows you to specify a color bar to be put in the beginning of the message to identify the following states:
    - **Good**: Green bar
    - **Normal**: No bar
    - **Warning**: Yellow bar
    - **Danger**: Red bar
- `icon_url`: This allows you to change the user image for that message

# Rocket Chat

Many companies like the functionality of Slack, but have problems to tradeoff the privacy that an on-premises service gives you for the Slack functionality. Rocket Chat is open source software that implements most of the features of Slack, as well as the majority of its interface. Being open source, every company can install it on-premises and manage it in a way that is compliant with their IT rules.

As Rocket Chat's goal is to be a drop-in replacement for Slack, from our point of view, very few changes need to be done, in fact, we can create the file `uptime_and_rocket.yaml` with the following content:

```
- hosts: localhost
  tasks:
  - name: Read the machine uptime
```

```
        command: 'uptime -p'
        register: uptime
      - name: Send the uptime to rocketchat channel
        rocketchat:
          token: TOKEN
          domain: chat.example.com
          channel: '#ansible'
          msg: 'Local system uptime is {{ uptime.stdout }}.'
```

As you can see, the only lines that changed are the 6th and 7th, where the word `slack` has been replaced by `rocketchat`. Also, we need to add the domain field specifying where our installation of Rocket Chat is located.

Run the code with the following:

```
ansible-playbook -i localhost, uptime_and_rocketchat.yaml
```

This results in the following output:

```
PLAY [localhost] ********************************************
TASK [setup] ************************************************
ok: [localhost]

TASK [Read the machine uptime] ******************************
changed: [localhost]

TASK [Send the uptime to rocketchat channel] ****************
changed: [localhost]

PLAY RECAP **************************************************
localhost              : ok=3    changed=2    unreachable=0    failed=0
```

# Internet Relay Chat (IRC)

IRC is probably the most well-known and widely-used chat protocol of the 1990s and it's still used today, mainly due to its use in open source communities and its simplicity. From an Ansible perspective, IRC is a pretty straightforward module and we can use it as in the following example (to be put in the `uptime_and_irc.yaml` file):

```
- hosts: localhost
  tasks:
  - name: Read the machine uptime
    command: 'uptime -p'
    register: uptime
  - name: Send the uptime to IRC channel
```

```yaml
      irc:
        port: 6669
        server: irc.example.net
        channel: #desired_channel
        msg: 'Local system uptime is {{ uptime.stdout }}.'
        color: green
```

 You need the `socket` Python library installed to use the Ansible IRC module.

In the IRC module, the following fields are required:

- `channel`: This is to specify in which channel your message will be delivered
- `msg`: This is the message you want to send

Other configurations you will usually specify are:

- `server`: Select `server` to connect to, if not `localhost`
- `port`: Select `port` to connect to, if not `6667`
- `color`: This to specify the message `color`, if not `black`
- `nick`: This to specify the `nick` sending the message, if not `ansible`
- `use_ssl`: Use SSL and TLS security
- `style`: If you want to send your message with bold, italic, underline, or reverse style

Run the code with the following:

```
ansible-playbook uptime_and_irc.yaml
```

This results in the following output:

```
PLAY [localhost] **********************************************
TASK [setup] **************************************************
ok: [localhost]

TASK [Read the machine uptime] ********************************
changed: [localhost]

TASK [Send the uptime to IRC channel] *************************
changed: [localhost]

PLAY RECAP ****************************************************
localhost              : ok=3    changed=2    unreachable=0    failed=0
```

# Amazon Simple Notification Service

Sometimes, you want your playbooks to be agnostic in the way you receive the alert. This has several advantages, mainly in terms of flexibility. In fact, in this model, Ansible will deliver the messages to a notification service and the notification service will then take care of delivering them. **Amazon Simple Notification Service (SNS)** is not the only notification service available, but it's probably the most used. SNS has the following components:

- **Messages**: Messages generated by publishers identified by a UUID
- **Publishers**: Programs generating messages
- **Topics**: Named groups of messages, which can be thought of in a similar way to chat channels or rooms
- **Subscribers**: Clients that will receive all messages published in the topics they have subscribed to

So in our case, we will have, specifically:

- **Messages**: Ansible notifications
- **Publishers**: Ansible itself
- **Topics**: Probably different topics to group messages based on the system and/or the kind of notification (for example, storage, networking, computing)
- **Subscribers**: The people in your team that has to be notified

As we said, one of the big advantages of SNS is that you can decouple between the way Ansible sends messages (SNS API) and the way your users will receive the messages. In fact, you will be able to choose different delivery systems per user and per topic rules, and eventually you can change them dynamically to ensure that the messages are sent in the best way possible for any situation. The five ways SNS can send messages, at the moment, are:

- Amazon **lambda** functions (serverless functions written in Python, Java, and JavaScript)
- Amazon **Simple Queue Service** (**SQS**) (a message queueing system)
- E-mail
- HTTP(S) call
- SMS

*Getting Notifications from Ansible*

Let's see how we can send SNS messages with Ansible. To do so, we can create a file called `uptime_and_sns.yaml` with the following content:

```yaml
- hosts: localhost
  tasks:
  - name: Read the machine uptime
    command: 'uptime -p'
    register: uptime
  - name: Send the uptime to SNS
    sns:
       msg: 'Local system uptime is {{ uptime.stdout }}.'
       subject: "System uptime"
       topic: "uptime"
```

In this example, we are using the `msg` key to set the message that will be sent, the `topic` to choose the most appropriate topic, and `subject` that will be used as the subject for e-mail deliveries. There are many other options you can set. Mainly, they are useful for sending different messages using different delivery methods. For instance, it would make sense to send a short message via SMS (in the end, the first S in SMS means **short**) and longer and more detailed messages via e-mails. To do so, the SNS module provides us with the following delivery-specific options:

- E-mail
- HTTP
- HTTPS
- SMS
- SQS

This module allows us also to set three AWS-specific parameters that I've not specified because I have a configuration file for AWS credentials and options:

- `aws_access_key`: AWS access key, if not specified the environmental variable, `aws_access_key` will be considered or the content of `~/.aws/credentials`
- `aws_secret_key`: AWS secret key, if not specified the environmental variable, `aws_secret_key` will be considered or the content of `~/.aws/credentials`
- `region`: AWS region to use, if not specified the environmental variable, `ec2_region` will be considered or the content of `~/.aws/config`

Run the code with the following command:

```
ansible-playbook uptime_and_sns.yaml
```

This will result in the following output:

```
PLAY [localhost] *********************************************

TASK [setup] *************************************************
ok: [localhost]


TASK [Read the machine uptime] *******************************
changed: [localhost]


TASK [Send the uptime to SNS] ********************************
changed: [localhost]


PLAY RECAP ***************************************************
localhost         : ok=3    changed=2    unreachable=0    failed=0
```

# Nagios

Nagios is one of the most used tools for controlling the status of services and servers. Nagios is capable of regularly auditing the state of servers and services, and notifying users in case of problems. If you have Nagios in your environment, you need to be very careful when you administer your machines, because in cases where Nagios finds servers or services in an unhealthy state, it will start sending e-mails, SMS messages, and calls to your whole team. When you run Ansible scripts against nodes that are controlled by Nagios you have to be even more careful, because you risk e-mails, SMS messages, and calls being triggered during the night or other inappropriate times. To avoid this, Ansible is able to notify Nagios beforehand, so that Nagios does not send notifications in that time window even if some services are down (for instance, because they are rebooted) or other checks fail.

In this example, we are going to stop a service, wait for 5 minutes, then start it again since this would actually create a Nagios failure in the majority of configurations. In fact, usually, Nagios is configured to accept up to two consecutive failures of a test (with usually one execution every minute) putting the service in a warning state before raising a critical state. We are going to create the file, `long_restart_service.yaml` which will trigger the Nagios critical state:

```
- hosts: ws01.fale.io
  tasks:
  - name: Stop the HTTPd service
    service:
      name: httpd
```

# Getting Notifications from Ansible

```
        state: stopped
      - name: Wait for 5 minutes
        pause:
          minutes: 5
      - name: Start the HTTPd service
        service:
          name: httpd
          state: stopped
```

Run the code with the following:

```
ansible-playbook long_restart_service.yaml
```

This should trigger a Nagios alert and result in the following output:

```
PLAY [ws01.fale.io] *******************************************

TASK [setup] **************************************************
ok: [ws01.fale.io]


TASK [Stop the HTTpd service] *********************************
changed: [ws01.fale.io]


TASK [Wait for 5 minutes] *************************************
changed: [ws01.fale.io]


TASK [Start the HTTpd service] ********************************
changed: [ws01.fale.io]


PLAY RECAP ****************************************************
ws01.fale.io        : ok=4    changed=3    unreachable=0    failed=0
```

If no Nagios alert has been triggered, either your Nagios installation probably does not track that service, or 5 minutes is not enough to make it raise a critical state.

We can now create a very similar playbook that will ensure that Nagios will not send any alerts. We are going to create a file called `long_restart_service_no_alert.yaml` with the following content:

```
- hosts: ws01.fale.io
  tasks:
  - name: Silence Nagios
```

```yaml
      nagios:
        action: disable_alerts
        service: httpd
        host: '{{ inventory_hostname }}'
      delegate_to: nagios.fale.io
    - name: Stop the HTTPd service
      service:
        name: httpd
        state: stopped
    - name: Wait for 5 minutes
      pause:
        minutes: 5
    - name: Start the HTTPd service
      service:
        name: httpd
        state: stopped
    - name: Desilence Nagios
      nagios:
        action: enable_alerts
        service: httpd
        host: '{{ inventory_hostname }}'
      delegate_to: nagios.fale.io
```

As you can see, we have added two tasks. The first to inform Nagios not to send alerts for the HTTPd service on the given host, and the second to inform Nagios to start sending alerts for the service again. Even if you do not specify the service and therefore all alerts on that host are silenced, my advice is to disable only the alert you are going to break so that Nagios is still able to work normally on the majority of your infrastructure.

 If the playbook run fails before reaching the re-enablement of the alerts, your alerts will stay *disabled*.

This module's goal is to toggle the Nagios alerts as well as schedule downtime, and from Ansible 2.2 this module can also unscheduled downtimes.

Run the code with the following command:

```
ansible-playbook long_restart_service_no_alert.yaml
```

This should trigger a Nagios alert and result in the following output:

```
PLAY [ws01.fale.io] *********************************************
TASK [setup] ****************************************************
ok: [ws01.fale.io]
```

```
TASK [Silence Nagios] ******************************************
changed: [nagios.fale.io]

TASK [Stop the HTTpd service] **********************************
changed: [ws01.fale.io]

TASK [Wait for 5 minutes] **************************************
changed: [ws01.fale.io]

TASK [Start the HTTpd service] *********************************
changed: [ws01.fale.io]

TASK [Desilence Nagios] ****************************************
changed: [nagios.fale.io]

PLAY RECAP *****************************************************
ws01.fale.io        : ok=4    changed=3    unreachable=0    failed=0
nagios.fale.io      : ok=2    changed=2    unreachable=0    failed=0
```

To use the Nagios module, you need to delegate the action to your Nagios server.

Sometimes, what you want to achieve with a Nagios integration is exactly the opposite, in fact, you are not interested to silentiate it, but you want Nagios to handle your test results. A common case is if you want to leverage your Nagios configuration to notify your administrators of the output of a task. To do so, we can use the Nagios nsca utility, integrating it into our playbooks. Ansible does not yet have a specific module for managing it, but you can always run it using the command module, leveraging the send_nsca CLI program.

## Summary

In this chapter, we have seen how we can teach Ansible how to send notifications to other systems and/or people.

In the next chapter, we will learn how to create a module so that you can extend Ansible to perform any kind of task.

# 7
# Creating a Custom Module

This chapter will focus on how to write and test custom modules. We've already discussed how modules work and how to use them within your tasks. Well, just for a quick recap, a module in Ansible is a piece of code, which is transferred and executed on your remote host every time you run an Ansible task (it can also run locally if you've used `local_action`).

From my experience, I've seen custom modules being written whenever a certain functionality needs to be exposed as a first-class task. The same functionality could have been achieved without the module, but it would have required a series of tasks with existing modules to accomplish the end goal and often also command and shell modules. For example, let's say you wanted to provision a server via **Preboot Execution Environment** (**PXE**). Without a custom module, you would have probably used a few shell or command tasks to accomplish the same. However, with a custom module, you would just pass the required parameters to it and the business logic will be embedded within the custom module in order to perform the PXE boot. This gives you the ability to write playbooks that are much simpler to read and a bigger reusability of the code, since you create the module once and you can use it everywhere, in your roles and playbooks.

The arguments that you pass to a module, provided they are in a key-value format, will be forwarded in a separate file along with the module. Ansible expects at least two variables in your module output, (that is, the result of the module run) whether it passed or failed, and a message for the user, and they both have to be in the JSON format. If you adhere to this simple rule, you can customize as much as you want!

# Creating a Custom Module

In this chapter, we will cover the following topics:

- Python modules
- Bash modules
- Ruby modules
- Testing modules

When you choose a particular technology or tool, you generally start with what it offers. You slowly understand the philosophy behind building the tool and what problems it helps you solve. However, you truly feel comfortable and in control only when you understand in depth how it works. At some stage, to utilize the complete power of a tool, you'll have to customize it in ways and means that suit your particular needs. Over a period of time, tools that provide you with an easy way to plug in new functionalities stay, and those that don't, disappear from the market. It's a similar story with Ansible as well. All tasks in Ansible playbooks are modules of some kind and it comes loaded with hundreds of modules. You will find a module for almost everything you might need. However, there are always exceptions. This is where the power to extend it comes in.

Chef provides **Lightweight Resources and Providers** (**LWRPs**) to perform this activity and Ansible allows you to extend its functionality using custom modules. The significant difference, however, is that you can write the module in any language of your choice (provided you have an interpreter of that language), whereas in Chef, the module has to be in Ruby. Ansible developers recommend using Python for any complex module, as there is out-of-the-box support to parse arguments; almost all ***nix** systems have Python installed by default and Ansible itself is written in Python. To be complete, in this chapter we will also see how you can write modules in other languages.

To make your custom modules available to Ansible, you can do one of the following:

- Specify the path to your custom module in the environment variable `ANSIBLE_LIBRARY`
- Use the `--module-path` command-line option
- Drop the modules in the `library` directory in your Ansible top-level directory

With this background information, let's look at some code!

## Using Python modules

Ansible intends to allow users to write modules in any language. Writing the module in Python, however, has its own advantages. You can take advantage of Ansible's libraries to shorten your code, an advantage not available for modules in other languages. Parsing user arguments, handling errors, and returning the required values becomes easier with the help of the Ansible libraries. We will see two examples for a custom Python module, one with and one without using the Ansible library, to give you a glimpse of how custom modules work. Make sure you organize your directory structure as mentioned in the previous section before creating the module. The first example creates a module named `check_user`. To do so, we will need to create the `check_user` file in the `library` folder within the Ansible top-level directory, with the following content:

```python
#!/usr/bin/env python

import pwd
import sys
import shlex
import json

def main():
    # Parsing argument file
    args = {}
    args_file = sys.argv[1]
    args_data = file(args_file).read()
    arguments = shlex.split(args_data)
    for arg in arguments:
        if '=' in arg:
            (key, value) = arg.split('=')
            args[key] = value
    user = args['user']

    # Check if user exists
    try:
        pwd.getpwnam(user)
        success = True
        ret_msg = 'User %s exists' % user
    except KeyError:
        success = False
        ret_msg = 'User %s does not exists' % user

    # Error handling and JSON return
    if success:
        print json.dumps({
            'msg': ret_msg
        })
```

## Creating a Custom Module

```
            sys.exit(0)
    else:
        print json.dumps({
            'failed': True,
            'msg': ret_msg
        })
        sys.exit(1)
main()
```

The preceding custom module, `check_user`, will check whether a user exists on a host. The module expects a user argument from Ansible. Let's break down the preceding module and see what it does. We first declare the **Interpreter** (Python) and import the libraries required to parse the arguments:

```
#!/usr/bin/env python

import pwd
import sys
import shlex
import json
```

Using the `sys` library, we then parse the arguments, which are passed in a file by Ansible. The arguments are in the format `param1=value1 param2=value2` where `param1` and `param2` are parameters and `value1` and `value2` are values of the parameters. There are multiple ways to split arguments and create a dictionary and we've chosen an easy way to perform the operation. We first create a list of arguments by splitting the arguments with a whitespace character, and then separate the key and value by splitting the arguments with an = character and assigning it to a Python dictionary. For example, if you have a string such as `user=foo gid=1000`, then you will first create a list, which will look like `["user=foo", "gid=1000"]` and then loop over this list to create a dictionary. This dictionary will look like `{"user": "foo", "gid": 1000}`. This is performed by the following lines:

```
def main():
    # Parsing argument file
    args = {}
    args_file = sys.argv[1]
    args_data = file(args_file).read()
    arguments = shlex.split(args_data)
    for arg in arguments:
        if '=' in arg:
            (key, value) = arg.split('=')
            args[key] = value
    user = args['user']
```

*Chapter 7*

 We separate the arguments based on a whitespace character because this is the standard followed by core Ansible modules. You can use any separator instead of a whitespace, but we would encourage you to maintain uniformity.

Once we have the user argument, we then check whether that user exists on the host as follows:

```
# Check if user exists
try:
    pwd.getpwnam(user)
    success = True
    ret_msg = 'User %s exists' % user
except KeyError:
    success = False
    ret_msg = 'User %s does not exists' % user
```

We use the `pwd` library to check the `passwd` file for the user. For the sake of simplicity, we use two variables: one to store the success or failure message and the other to store the message for the user. Finally, we use the variables created in the `try-catch` block to check if the module succeeded or failed, as you can see in this snippet:

```
# Error handling and JSON return
if success:
    print json.dumps({
        'msg': ret_msg
    })
    sys.exit(0)
else:
    print json.dumps({
        'failed': True,
        'msg': ret_msg
    })
    sys.exit(1)
```

If the module succeeds, then we will exit the execution with an exit code 0 [`exit(0)`]; else, we will exit with a non-zero code. Ansible will look for the failed variable and if it is set to `True`, it will exit unless you have explicitly asked Ansible to ignore errors using the `ignore_errors` parameter. You can use customized modules like any other core module of Ansible. To test the custom module, we will need a playbook, so let's create the file `playbooks/check_user.yaml` with the following content:

```
- hosts: localhost
  vars:
    user_ok: root
    user_ko: this_user_does_not_exists
```

# Creating a Custom Module

```yaml
    tasks:
      - name: 'Check if user {{ user_ok }} exists'
        check_user:
          user: '{{ user_ok }}'
      - name: 'Check if user {{ user_ko }} exists'
        check_user:
          user: '{{ user_ko }}'
```

As you can see, we used the `check_user` module like any other core module. Ansible will execute this module on the remote host by copying the module to the remote host with arguments in a separate file. Let's see how this playbook runs with the following:

**ansible-playbook playbooks/check_user.yaml**

We should receive the following output:

```
PLAY [localhost] ***************************************************
TASK [setup] *******************************************************
ok: [localhost]

TASK [Check if user root exists] **********************************
ok: [localhost]

TASK [Check if user this_user_does_not_exists exists] ************
fatal: [localhost]: FAILED! => {"changed": false, "failed": true,
"msg": "User this_user_does_not_exists does not exists"}

NO MORE HOSTS LEFT ************************************************
     to retry, use: --limit @playbooks/check_user.retry

PLAY RECAP *********************************************************
localhost              : ok=2    changed=0    unreachable=0    failed=1
```

As expected, since we have the `root` user, but not the `this_user_does_not_exists`, it passed the first check, but failed at the second.

Ansible also provides a Python library to parse user arguments and handle errors and returns. It's time to see how the Ansible Python library is useful to make your code shorter, faster, and less error prone. To do so, let's create a file called `library/check_user_py2.py` with the following content:

```python
#!/usr/bin/env python

import pwd
from ansible.module_utils.basic import AnsibleModule

def main():
```

```python
    # Parsing argument file
    module = AnsibleModule(
        argument_spec = dict(
            user = dict(required=True)
        )
    )
    user = module.params.get('user')

    # Check if user exists
    try:
        pwd.getpwnam(user)
        success = True
        ret_msg = 'User %s exists' % user
    except KeyError:
        success = False
        ret_msg = 'User %s does not exists' % user

    # Error handling and JSON return
    if success:
        module.exit_json(msg=ret_msg)
    else:
        module.fail_json(msg=ret_msg)

if __name__ == "__main__":
    main()
```

Let's break down the preceding module and see how it works, as follows:

```python
#!/usr/bin/env python

import pwd
from ansible.module_utils.basic import AnsibleModule
```

As you can see, we do not import `sys`, `shlex` and `json`; we are not using them anymore, since all the operations that required them are now done by Ansible `module_utils`.

```python
    # Parsing argument file
    module = AnsibleModule(
        argument_spec = dict(
            user = dict(required=True)
        )
    )
    user = module.params.get('user')
```

# Creating a Custom Module

Previously, we performed a lot of processing on the argument file to get the final user arguments. Ansible makes it easy by providing an `AnsibleModule` class, which does all the processing on its own and provides us with the final arguments. The `required=True` parameter means that the argument is mandatory and the execution will fail if the argument is not passed. The default value for required is `False`, which will allow users to skip the argument. You can then access the value of the arguments through the `module.params` dictionary by calling the `get` method on `module.params`. The logic to check users on the remote host will remain the same, but the error handling and return aspect will change as follows:

```
# Error handling and JSON return
if success:
    module.exit_json(msg=ret_msg)
else:
    module.fail_json(msg=ret_msg)
```

One of the advantages of using the `AnsibleModule` object, is that you have very nice facility to handle returning values to the playbook. We will go into more depth in the next section.

> We could have condensed the logic to check user and the return section, but we kept them divided for readability.

To verify that everything works as expected, we can create a new playbook in `playbooks/check_user_py2.yaml` with the following content:

```
- hosts: localhost
  vars:
    user_ok: root
    user_ko: this_user_does_not_exists
  tasks:
  - name: 'Check if user {{ user_ok }} exists'
    check_user_py2:
      user: '{{ user_ok }}'
  - name: 'Check if user {{ user_ko }} exists'
    check_user_py2:
      user: '{{ user_ko }}'
```

Run it with the following:

**ansible-playbook playbooks/check_user.yaml**

We should receive the following output:

```
PLAY [localhost] *********************************************
TASK [setup] *************************************************
ok: [localhost]

TASK [Check if user root exists] *****************************
ok: [localhost]

TASK [Check if user this_user_does_not_exists exists] ********
fatal: [localhost]: FAILED! => {"changed": false, "failed": true,
"msg": "User this_user_does_not_exists does not exists"}

NO MORE HOSTS LEFT *******************************************
    to retry, use: --limit @playbooks/check_user_py2.retry

PLAY RECAP ***************************************************
localhost            : ok=2    changed=0    unreachable=0    failed=1
```

Which is consistent with our expectations.

## Working with exit_json and fail_json

Ansible provides a shorter way to handle success and failure by providing the exit_json and fail_json methods, respectively. You can directly pass a message to these methods and Ansible will take care of the rest. You can also pass additional variables to these methods and Ansible will print those variables to stdout. For example, apart from the message, you might also want to print the uid and gid parameters of the user. You can do this by passing these variables to the exit_json method separated by a comma.

Let's see how you can return multiple values to stdout, which is demonstrated in the following code placed in library/check_user_id.py:

```python
#!/usr/bin/env python

import pwd
from ansible.module_utils.basic import AnsibleModule

class CheckUser:
    def __init__(self, user):
        self.user = user

    # Check if user exists
    def check_user(self):
        uid = ''
        gid = ''
        try:
```

```python
                user = pwd.getpwnam(self.user)
                success = True
                ret_msg = 'User %s exists' % self.user
                uid = user.pw_uid
                gid = user.pw_gid
            except KeyError:
                success = False
                ret_msg = 'User %s does not exists' % self.user
            return success, ret_msg, uid, gid

    def main():
        # Parsing argument file
        module = AnsibleModule(
            argument_spec = dict(
                user = dict(required=True)
            )
        )
        user = module.params.get('user')

        chkusr = CheckUser(user)
        success, ret_msg, uid, gid = chkusr.check_user()

        # Error handling and JSON return
        if success:
            module.exit_json(msg=ret_msg, uid=uid, gid=gid)
        else:
            module.fail_json(msg=ret_msg)

    if __name__ == "__main__":
        main()
```

As you can see, we return the `uid` and `gid` of the user along with the message, `msg`. You can have multiple values and Ansible will print all of them in a dictionary format. We can create a playbook in `playbooks/check_user_id.yaml` with the following content:

```yaml
- hosts: localhost
  vars:
    user: root
  tasks:
  - name: 'Retrive {{ user }} data if it exists'
    check_user_id:
      user: '{{ user }}'
    register: user_data
  - name: 'Print user {{ user }} data'
    debug:
      msg: '{{ user_data }}'
```

Run it with the following:

```
ansible-playbook playbooks/check_user.yaml
```

We should receive the following output:

```
PLAY [localhost] **********************************************
TASK [setup] **************************************************
ok: [localhost]

TASK [Retrieve fale data if it exists] ************************
ok: [localhost]

TASK [Print user fale data] ***********************************
ok: [localhost] => {
    "msg": {
        "changed": false,
        "gid": 1000,
        "msg": "User root exists",
        "uid": 1000
    }
}

PLAY RECAP ****************************************************
localhost          : ok=3    changed=0    unreachable=0    failed=0
```

## Testing Python modules

As we have seen, you can test your modules creating very simple playbooks that run them. You can also test your module by running it more directly. To do so, we'll need to clone the Ansible official repository (if you haven't done it yet):

```
git clone git://github.com/ansible/ansible.git --recursive
```

Source an environmental file:

```
source ansible/hacking/env-setup
```

We can now use the `test-module` utility to run the script passing the filename as a command-line argument:

```
ansible/hacking/test-module -m library/check_user_id.py -a "user=root"
```

The result will be something like this:

```
* including generated source, if any, saving to:
/home/fale/.ansible_module_generated
```

# Creating a Custom Module

```
    * ansiballz module detected; extracted module source to:
/home/fale/debug_dir
    *********************************
    RAW OUTPUT

    {"msg": "User root exists", "invocation": {"module_args": {"user":
"root"}}, "gid":       0, "uid": 0, "changed": false}


    *********************************
    PARSED OUTPUT
    {
        "changed": false,
        "gid": 0,
        "invocation": {
            "module_args": {
                "user": "root"
            }
        },
        "msg": "User root exists",
        "uid": 0
    }
```

It's also simple to execute the script directly, if you have not used the `AnsibleModule`, this is due the fact that this module requires lots of Ansible-specific variables, so it's more complex to "simulate" an Ansible run than to actually run Ansible itself.

## Using bash modules

Bash modules in Ansible are no different than any other bash scripts, except the way it prints the data on `stdout`. Bash modules could be as simple as checking if a process is running on the remote host to running some complex commands.

As previously stated, the general recommendation is to use Python for modules. In my opinion the second-best choice (only for very easy modules) is `bash` module due to its simplicity and user base.

Let's create the file `library/kill_java.sh` with the following content:

```
#!/bin/bash
source $1
```

```
    SERVICE=$service_name

    JAVA_PIDS=$(/usr/java/default/bin/jps | grep ${SERVICE} | awk '{print
$1}')

    if [ ${JAVA_PIDS} ]; then
        for JAVA_PID in ${JAVA_PIDS}; do
            /usr/bin/kill -9 ${JAVA_PID}
        done
        echo "failed=False msg="Killed all the orphaned processes for
${SERVICE}""
        exit 0
    else
        echo "failed=False msg="No orphaned processes to kill for
${SERVICE}""
        exit 0
    fi
```

The preceding `bash` module will take the `service_name` argument and forcefully kill all of the Java processes that belong to that service. As you know, Ansible passes the argument file to the module. We then source the arguments file using source `$1`. This will actually set the environment variable with the name, `service_name`. We then access this variable using `$service_name` as follows:

```
source $1

SERVICE=$service_name
```

We then check to see if we obtained any PIDs for the service and run a loop over it to forcefully kill all of the Java processes that match `service_name`. Once they're killed, we exit the module with `failed=False` and a message with an exit code of 0, as you can see here:

```
    if [ ${JAVA_PIDS} ]; then
        for JAVA_PID in ${JAVA_PIDS}; do
            /usr/bin/kill -9 ${JAVA_PID}
        done
        echo "failed=False msg="Killed all the orphaned processes for
${SERVICE}""
        exit 0
```

If we do not find any running process for the service, we will still exit the module with an exit code of 0 because terminating the Ansible run might not make sense; this is in the following part:

```
    else
        echo "failed=False msg="No orphaned processes to kill for
```

# Creating a Custom Module

```
${SERVICE}""
        exit 0
    fi
```

 You can also terminate the Ansible run by printing `failed=True` with an exit code of `1`.

Ansible allows you to return a key-value output if the language itself doesn't support JSON. This makes Ansible more developer/sysadmin-friendly and allows custom modules to be written in any language of one's choice. Let's test the `bash` module by passing the arguments file to the module. We can now create an arguments file in `/tmp/arguments` that has the `service_name` parameter set to Jenkins, as follows:

```
service_name=jenkins
```

Now, you can run the module like any other bash script. Let's see what happens when we run it with:

**bash library/kill_java.sh /tmp/arguments**

We should receive the following output:

**failed=False msg="No orphaned processes to kill for jenkins"**

As expected, the module did not fail even though there was no Jenkins process running on the localhost.

## Using Ruby modules

Writing modules in Ruby is as easy as writing a module in Python or bash. You just need to take care of the arguments, errors, return statements, and of course, know basic Ruby! Let's create the `library/rsync.rb` file with the following code:

```ruby
#!/usr/bin/env ruby

require 'rsync'
require 'json'

src = ''
dest = ''
ret_msg = ''
SUCCESS = ''
```

```ruby
def print_message(state, mdg, key='Failed')
    message = {
        key => state,
        "msg" => msg
    }
    print message.to_json
    exit 1 if state == false
    exit 0
end

args_file = ARGV[0]
data = File.read(args_file)
arguments = data.split(" ")
arguments.each do |argument|
    print_message(false, "Argument should be name-value pairs. Example name=foo") if not argument.include("=")
    field.value = argument.split("=")
    if field == "src"
        src = value
    elseif field == "dest"
        dest = value
    else print_message(false, "Invalid argument provided. Valid arguments are src and dest.")
    end
end

result - Rsync.run("#{src}", "#{dest}")
if result.success?
    success = true
    ret_msg = "Copied file successfully"
else
    success = false
    ret_msg = result.error
end

if success
    print_message(false, "#{ret_msg}")
else
    print_message(true, "#{ret_msg}")
end
```

In the preceding module, we first process the user arguments, then copy the file using the `rsync` library, and finally, return the output. Let's break down the preceding code and see how it works.

## Creating a Custom Module

We first wrote a method, `print_message`, which will print the output in a JSON format. By doing this, we can reuse the same code in multiple places. Remember, the output of your module should contain `failed=true` if you want the Ansible run to fail; otherwise, Ansible will think that the module succeeded and will continue with the next task. The output obtained is as follows:

```ruby
#!/usr/bin/env ruby

require 'rsync'
require 'json'

src = ''
dest = ''
ret_msg = ''
SUCCESS = ''

def print_message(state, mdg, key='Failed')
    message = {
        key => state,
        "msg" => msg
    }
    print message.to_json
    exit 1 if state == false
    exit 0
end
```

We then process the arguments file, which contains a key-value pair separated by a whitespace character. This is similar to what we did with the Python module earlier, where we took care of parsing out the arguments. We also perform some checks to make sure that the user has not missed any required argument. In this case, we check if the `src` and `dest` parameters have been specified and print a message if the arguments are not provided. Further checks could include the format and type of arguments. You can add these checks and any other checks you deem important. For example, if one of your parameters is a `date`, then you'd like to verify that the input is actually the right date. Consider the following piece of code, which shows the discussed parameters:

```ruby
args_file = ARGV[0]
data = File.read(args_file)
arguments = data.split(" ")
arguments.each do |argument|
    print_message(false, "Argument should be name-value pairs. Example name=foo") if not argument.include("=")
        field.value = argument.split("=")
        if field == "src"
            src = value
        elseif field == "dest"
```

```
            dest = value
        else print_message(false, "Invalid argument provided. Valid
arguments are src and dest.")
        end
    end
end
```

Once we have the required arguments, we will go ahead and copy the file using the `rsync` library as follows:

```
result - Rsync.run("#{src}", "#{dest}")
if result.success?
    success = true
    ret_msg = "Copied file successfully"
else
    success = false
    ret_msg = result.error
end
```

Finally, we check if the `rsync` task passed or failed and call the `print_message` function to print the output on `stdout` as follows:

```
if success
    print_message(false, "#{ret_msg}")
else
    print_message(true, "#{ret_msg}")
end
```

You can test your Ruby module by simply passing the arguments file to the module. To do so, we can create the file /tmp/arguments with the following content:

```
src=/var/log/ansible.log dest=/tmp/ansible_backup.log
```

Let's now run the module, as shown:

**ruby library/rsync.rb /tmp/arguments**

We will receive the following output:

```
{"failed":false,"msg":"Copied file successfully"}
```

We will leave the `serverspec` testing for you to complete.

*Creating a Custom Module*

# Testing modules

Testing is often undervalued due to lack of understanding of its purpose and the benefits it can bring to the business. Testing modules is as important as testing any other part of the Ansible playbook because a small change in a module can break your entire playbook. We will take an example of the Python module that we wrote in the first section of this chapter and write an integration test using Python's nose test framework. Unit tests are also encouraged, but for our scenario where we check if a user exists remotely, an integration test makes more sense.

nose is a Python test framework. For more information, visit https://nose.readthedocs.org/en/latest/.

To test the module, we convert our previous module into a Python class so that we can directly import the class in our test, and run only the main logic of the module. The following code shows the library/check_user_py3.py restructured module, which will check whether a user exists on a remote host:

```python
#!/usr/bin/env python

import pwd
from ansible.module_utils.basic import AnsibleModule

class User:
    def __init__(self, user):
        self.user = user

    # Check if user exists
    def check_if_user_exists(self):
        try:
            user = pwd.getpwnam(self.user)
            success = True
            ret_msg = 'User %s exists' % self.user
        except KeyError:
            success = False
            ret_msg = 'User %s does not exists' % self.user
        return success, ret_msg

def main():
    # Parsing argument file
    module = AnsibleModule(
        argument_spec = dict(
            user = dict(required=True)
```

```
            )
        )
        user = module.params.get('user')

        chkusr = User(user)
        success, ret_msg = chkusr.check_if_user_exists()

        # Error handling and JSON return
        if success:
            module.exit_json(msg=ret_msg, uid=uid, gid=gid)
        else:
            module.fail_json(msg=ret_msg)

if __name__ == "__main__":
    main()
```

As you can see in the preceding code, we created a class named User. We instantiated the class, and called the check_if_user_exists method to check if the user actually exists on the remote machine. It's time to write an integration test now. We assume that you have the nose package installed on your system. If not, don't worry! You can still install the package by using the following command:

**pip install nose**

Let's now write the integration test file in library/test_check_user_py3.py as follows:

```
from nose.tools import assert_equals, assert_false, assert_true
import imp
imp.load_source("check_user","check_user_py3.py")
from check_user import User

def test_check_user_positive():
    chkusr = User("root")
    success, ret_msg = chkusr.check_if_user_exists()
    assert_true(success)
    assert_equals('User root exists', ret_msg)

def test_check_user_negative():
    chkusr = User("this_user_does_not_exists")
    success, ret_msg = chkusr.check_if_user_exists()
    assert_false(success)
    assert_equals('User this_user_does_not_exists does not exists', ret_msg)
```

*Creating a Custom Module*

In the preceding integration test, we import the `nose` package and our module, `check_user`. We call the `User` class by passing the user we want to check. We then check whether the user exists on the remote host by calling the `check_if_user_exists()` method. The `nose` methods, `assert_true`, `assert_false`, and `assert_equals` can be used to compare the expected value against the actual. Only if the assert methods pass, will the test pass. You can have multiple tests inside the same file by having multiple methods whose names start with `test_`, for example, the `test_check_user_positive()` and `test_check_user_negative()` methods. Nose tests will take all the methods that start with `test_` and execute them.

As you can see, we actually created two tests for just one function. This is a key part of tests. Always try cases where you know it will work, but also do not forget to test cases where you expect it to fail.

We can now test if it works running nose in the following way:

```
cd library
nosetests -v test_check_users_py3.py
```

You should receive output similar to this:

```
test_check_user_py3.test_check_user_positive ... ok
test_check_user_py3.test_check_user_negative ... ok
----------------------------------------------------------------------
Ran 2 tests in 0.001s
OK
```

As you can see, the test passed because the `root` user existed on the host while the `this_user_does_not_exists` user does not exist.

We use the `-v` option with `nose` tests for the **verbose** mode.

For more complicated modules, we recommend that you write unit tests and integration tests. You might wonder why we didn't use `serverspec` to test the module.

[ 176 ]

We still recommend running `serverspec` tests for functional testing as part of playbooks, but for unit and integration tests, it's recommended to use well-known frameworks. Similarly, if you write Ruby modules, we recommend you write tests for them with a framework such as `rspec`. If your custom Ansible module has multiple parameters with multiple combinations, then you will write more tests to test each scenario. Finally, we recommend that your run all these tests as part of your CI system, be it Jenkins, Travis, or any other system.

Questions

A couple of questions to think about are given in the this section:

- Can you think of common tasks that you perform daily and how you would write Ansible modules for them? List them down in terms of how you would invoke the module from a playbook.
- Which language do you think your team would be comfortable using for your modules?
- Can you revisit the roles that you might have written after Chapter 3, *Scaling to Multiple Hosts*, and see which of them can potentially be converted into custom modules?

# Summary

With this, we come to the end of this rather small but important chapter, which focused on how you can extend Ansible by writing your own custom modules. You learned how to use Python, Bash, and Ruby in order to write your modules. We've also seen how to write integration tests for modules so that they can be integrated into your CI system. In future, hopefully, extending your Ansible functionality using modules should be way easier!

Next, we will step into the world of provisioning, deployment, and orchestration and look at how Ansible solves our infrastructure problems when we provision new instances or want to deploy software updates to various instances in our environments. We promise that the journey is going to be fun!

# 8
# Debugging and Error Handling

Like software code, testing infrastructure code is an all-important task. There should ideally be no code floating around in production that has not been tested, especially when you have strict customer SLAs to meet, and this is true even for the infrastructure. In this chapter, we'll look at syntactic checks, testing without applying the code on the machines (the no-op mode), and functional testing for playbooks, which are at the core of Ansible and trigger the various tasks you want to perform on the remote hosts. It is recommended that you integrate some of these into your **Continuous Integration** (**CI**) system that you have for Ansible to better test your playbooks. We'll be looking at the following points:

- Syntax checking
- Checking the mode with and without diff
- Functional testing

As part of functional testing, we will be looking at:

- Assertions on the end state of the system
- Testing with tags
- Serverspec (a different tool, but can work wonderfully with Ansible)
- Using the `--syntax-check` option

*Debugging and Error Handling*

Whenever you run a playbook, Ansible first checks the syntax of the playbook file. If an error is encountered, Ansible will error out saying there was a syntax error and will not proceed unless you fix that error. This syntax checking is performed only when you run the `ansible-playbook` command. When writing a big playbook or if you have included task files, it might be difficult to fix all of the errors; this might end up wasting more time. In order to deal with such situations, Ansible provides a way to check your YAML syntax as you keep progressing with your playbook. For this example, we will need to create the file `playbooks/setup_apache.yaml` with the following content:

```
- hosts: localhost
  tasks:
  - name: Install Apache
    yum:
      name: httpd
      state: present
  - name: Enable Apache
   service:
      name: httpd
      state: running
      enabled: True
```

Now that we have our example file, we need to run it with the `--syntax-check` parameter, so you will invoke Ansible as:

**ansible-playbook playbooks/setup_apache.yaml --syntax-check**

The `ansible-playbook` command checked the YAML syntax of the `setup_apache.yml` playbook and showed that the syntax of the playbook was correct. Let's look at the resulting errors from the invalid syntax in the playbook:

```
ERROR! Syntax Error while loading YAML.
   The error appears to have been in
'~/08_code/playbooks/setup_apache.yaml': line 9, column 4, but may
   be elsewhere in the file depending on the exact syntax problem.

The offending line appears to be:

 - name: Enable Apache
   service:
   ^ here
```

The error shows that there is an indentation error in the `Enable Apache` task. Ansible also gives you the line number, column number, and the filename where this error is found (even if this is not a guarantee of the exact location of the error). This should definitely be one of the basic tests that you should run as part of your CI for Ansible.

# The check mode

The check mode (also known as the **dry run** or **no-op mode**) will run your playbook in a no-operation mode, that is, it will not apply any changes to the remote host; instead, it will just show the changes that will be introduced when a task is run. Whether the check mode is actually enabled or not depends on each task. There are few commands that you may find interesting. All those modules will have to be run in `/usr/lib/python2.7/site-packages/ansible/modules` or where your Ansible module folder is (different paths could be possible based on the operating system you are using as well as the way you installed Ansible).

To count the number of available modules on your installation, you can perform this command:

```
find . -type f | grep '.py$' | grep -v '__init__' | wc -l
```

With Ansible 2.1.1, the result of this command is `569`, since Ansible has that many modules.

If you want to see how many of these support the check mode, you can run:

```
grep -r 'supports_check_mode=True' | awk -F: '{print $1}' | sort | uniq | wc -l
```

With Ansible 2.1.1 the result of this command is `242`.

You might also find the following command useful for listing all modules that support the check mode:

```
grep -r 'supports_check_mode=True' | awk -F: '{print $1}' | sort | uniq
```

*Debugging and Error Handling*

This helps you test how your playbook will behave and check if there may be any failures before running it on your production server. You run a playbook in the check mode by simply passing the `--check` option to your `ansible-playbook` command. Let's see how the check mode works with the `setup_apache.yml` playbook, as follows:

```
PLAY [localhost] ************************************************

TASK [setup] ****************************************************
ok: [localhost]

TASK [Install Apache] *******************************************
ok: [localhost]

TASK [Enable Apache] ********************************************
changed: [localhost]

PLAY RECAP ******************************************************
localhost            : ok=3    changed=1    unreachable=0    failed=0
```

In the preceding run, instead of making the changes on the target host, Ansible highlighted all the changes that would have occurred during the actual run. From the preceding run, you can find that `httpd` service was already installed on the target host, because of which, Ansible's exit message for that task was ok.

```
TASK [Install Apache] *******************************************
ok: [localhost]
```

Whereas, with the second task, it found that `httpd` service was not running on the target host:

```
TASK [Enable Apache] ********************************************
changed: [localhost]
```

When you run the preceding playbook again without the check mode enabled, Ansible will make sure that the service state is running.

# Indicating differences between files using --diff

In the check mode, you can use the `--diff` option to show the changes that would be applied to a file. To be able to see the `--diff` option in use, we need to change our `playbooks/setup_apache.yaml` playbook to match the following:

```
- hosts: localhost
  tasks:
  - name: Ensure Apache is installed
    yum:
      name: httpd
      state: present
  - name: Ensure Apache in enabled
    service:
      name: httpd
      state: running
      enabled: True
  - name: Ensure Apache userdirs are properly configured
    template:
      src: '../templates/userdir.conf'
      dest: '/etc/httpd/conf.d/userdir.conf'
```

As you can see, we added a task, which will ensure a certain state of the `/etc/httpd/conf.d/userdir.conf` file.

We also need to create a template file placed in `templates/userdir.conf` with the following content:

```
# UserDir: The name of the directory that is appended onto a user's home
# directory if a ~user request is received.
# The path to the end user account 'public_html' directory must be
# accessible to the webserver userid.  This usually means that ~userid
# must have permissions of 711, ~userid/public_html must have permissions
# of 755, and documents contained therein must be world-readable.
# Otherwise, the client will only receive a "403 Forbidden" message.
#
<IfModule mod_userdir.c>
    #
    # UserDir is disabled by default since it can confirm the presence
    # of a username on the system (depending on home directory
    # permissions).
    #
    UserDir enabled
```

## Debugging and Error Handling

```
        #
        # To enable requests to /~user/ to serve the user's public_html
        # directory, remove the "UserDir disabled" line above, and uncomment
        # the following line instead:
        #
        #UserDir public_html
    </IfModule>

    #
    # Control access to UserDir directories.  The following is an example
    # for a site where these directories are restricted to read-only.
    #
    <Directory "/home/*/public_html">
        AllowOverride FileInfo AuthConfig Limit Indexes
        Options MultiViews Indexes SymLinksIfOwnerMatch IncludesNoExec
        Require method GET POST OPTIONS
    </Directory>
```

In this template, we only changed the `UserDir enabled` line, which by default is `UserDir disabled`.

The `--diff` option doesn't work with the file module; you will have to use the template module only.

We can now test the result of this with the following command:

```
ansible-playbook playbooks/setup_apache.yaml --diff --check
```

As you can see, we are using the `--check` parameter that will ensure this will be a dry-run. We will receive the following output:

```
PLAY [localhost] ******************************************

TASK [setup] **********************************************
ok: [localhost]

TASK [Ensure Apache is installed] *************************
ok: [localhost]

TASK [Ensure Apache in enabled] ***************************
changed: [localhost]

TASK [Ensure Apache userdirs are properly configured] ************
```

```
changed: [localhost]
--- before: /etc/httpd/conf.d/userdir.conf
+++ after: dynamically generated
@@ -14,7 +14,7 @@
     # of a username on the system (depending on home directory
     # permissions).
     #
-    UserDir disabled
+    UserDir enabled

    #
    # To enable requests to /~user/ to serve the user's public_html
@@ -33,4 +33,3 @@
    Options MultiViews Indexes SymLinksIfOwnerMatch IncludesNoExec
    Require method GET POST OPTIONS
</Directory>
-

PLAY RECAP *************************************************************
localhost          : ok=4    changed=2    unreachable=0    failed=0
```

As we can see, Ansible compares the current file of the remote host with the source file; a line starting with + indicates that a line was added to the file, whereas - indicates that a line was removed.

 You can also use `--diff` without the `--check` option, which will allow Ansible to make the specified changes and show the difference between two files.

Using `--diff` and `--check` modes together is a test step that can potentially be used as part of your CI tests to assert how many steps have changed as part of the run. Another case where you can use those features together is the part of the deployment process that checks what exactly will change when you run Ansible on that machine.

There are also cases – that should not happen, but sometimes happen-where you have not run a playbook on a machine for a very long time and you are worried that running it again will break something. Using those options together should help you understand if it was just you worrying or if this is a real risk.

*Debugging and Error Handling*

# Functional testing in Ansible

Wikipedia says functional testing is a **Quality Assurance (QA) process** and a type of black-box testing that bases its test cases on the specifications of the software component under the test. **Functions are tested by feeding them input and examining the output**; the internal program structure is rarely considered. Functional testing is as important as code when it comes to infrastructure.

From an infrastructure perspective, with respect to functional testing, we test output of our Ansible runs on the actual machines. Ansible provides multiple ways to perform the functional testing of your playbook; let's look at some of the most commonly used methods.

# Functional testing using assert

The check mode will only work when you want to check whether a task will change anything on the host or not. This will not help when you want to check whether the output of your module is what you expected. For example, let's say you wrote a module that will check if a port is up or not. In order to test this, you might need to check the output of your module and see whether it matches the desired output or not. To perform such tests, Ansible provides a way to directly compare the output of a module with the desired output.

Let's see how this works creating the file `playbooks/assert_ls.yaml` with the following content:

```
- hosts: localhost
  tasks:
  - name: List files in /tmp
    command: ls /tmp
    register: list_files
  - name: Check if file testfile.txt exists
    assert:
      that:
        - "'testfile.txt' in list_files.stdout_lines"
```

In the preceding playbook, we're running the `ls` command on the target host and registering the output of that command in the `list_files` variable. Further, we ask Ansible to check whether the output of the `ls` command has the expected result. We do this using the `assert` module, which uses some conditional checks to verify if the `stdout` value of a task meets the expected output of the user. Let's run the preceding playbook to see what output Ansible returns with the command:

```
ansible-playbook playbooks/assert_ls.yaml
```

Since we don't have the file, we will receive the following output:

```
PLAY [localhost] **********************************************

TASK [setup] **************************************************
ok: [localhost]

TASK [List files in /tmp] *************************************
changed: [localhost]

TASK [Check if file testfile.txt exists] **********************
fatal: [localhost]: FAILED! => {"assertion": "'testfile.txt' in list_files.stdout_lines", "changed":     false, "evaluated_to": false, "failed": true}

NO MORE HOSTS LEFT ********************************************
    to retry, use: --limit @playbooks/assert_ls.retry

PLAY RECAP ****************************************************
localhost              : ok=2    changed=1   unreachable=0    failed=1
```

If we re-run the playbook after we create the expected file, it will not fail and therefore this will be the result:

```
PLAY [localhost] **********************************************

TASK [setup] **************************************************
ok: [localhost]

TASK [List files in /tmp] *************************************
changed: [localhost]

TASK [Check if file testfile.txt exists] **********************
ok: [localhost]

PLAY RECAP ****************************************************
localhost              : ok=3    changed=1   unreachable=0    failed=0
```

This time, the task passed with an ok message as `testfile.txt` was present in the `list_files` variable. Likewise, you can match multiple strings in a variable or multiple variables using the `and` and `or` operators. The assertion feature is quite powerful, and users who have written either unit or integration tests in their projects will be quite happy to see this feature!

# Testing with tags

Tags are a great way to test a bunch of tasks without running an entire playbook. We can use tags to run actual tests on the nodes to verify the state that the user intended to be in, the playbook. We can treat this as another way to run integration tests for Ansible on the actual box. The tag method to test can be run on the actual machines where you run Ansible, and also, it can be used primarily during deployments to test the state of your end systems. In this section, we'll first look at how to use tags in general, their features that can possibly help us, not just with testing but even otherwise, and finally for testing purposes.

To add tags in your playbook, use the tags parameter followed by one or more tag names separated by commas. Let's create a simple playbook in `playbooks/tags_example.yaml` to see how the tags work with the following content:

```yaml
- hosts: localhost
  tasks:
  - name: Ensure the file /tmp/ok exists
    file:
      name: /tmp/ok
      state: touch
    tags:
    - file_present
  - name: Ensure the file /tmp/ok does not exists
    file:
      name: /tmp/ok
      state: absent
    tags:
    - file_absent
```

If we now run the playbook, the file will be created and destroyed. We can see it running with the following command:

```
ansible-playbook playbooks/tags_example.yaml
```

It will give us this output:

```
PLAY [localhost] *******************************************************

TASK [setup] ***********************************************************
ok: [localhost]

TASK [Ensure the file /tmp/ok exists] **********************************
changed: [localhost]

TASK [Ensure the file /tmp/ok does not exists] *************************
changed: [localhost]
```

```
PLAY RECAP *************************************************
localhost              : ok=3    changed=2    unreachable=0    failed=0
```

Since this is not an idempotent playbook, if we run it over and over, we will always see the same result, as the playbook will create and delete the file every time.

You can now simply pass the `file_present` tag or the `file_absent` tag to only perform one of the actions, like in the following example:

```
ansible-playbook playbooks/tags_example.yaml -t file_present
```

Thanks to the `-t file_present` part, only the tasks with the `file_present` tag will be executed, in fact this will be the output:

```
PLAY [localhost] ********************************************

TASK [setup] ************************************************
ok: [localhost]

TASK [Ensure the file /tmp/ok exists] ***********************
changed: [localhost]

PLAY RECAP *************************************************
localhost              : ok=2    changed=1    unreachable=0    failed=0
```

You can also use tags to perform a set of tasks on the remote host just like taking a server out of a load balancer and adding it back to the load balancer.

You can also use the `--check` option with tags. By doing this, you can test your tasks without actually running them on your hosts. This allows you to test a bunch of individual tasks directly, instead of copying your tasks to a temporary playbook and running it from there.

# The --skip-tags

Ansible also provides a way to skip some tags in a playbook. If you have a long playbook with multiple tags, like 10, and you want to execute them all but one, then it would not be a good idea to pass nine tags to Ansible. The situation would be more difficult if you forgot to pass a tag and the `ansible-playbook` command fails. To overcome such situations, Ansible provides a way to skip a couple of tags, instead of passing multiple tags. It's functioning is pretty straightforward, and can be triggered in the following way:

```
ansible-playbook playbooks/tags_example.yaml --skip-tags file_present
```

The output will be something like:

```
PLAY [localhost] ************************************************

TASK [setup] ****************************************************
ok: [localhost]

TASK [Ensure the file /tmp/ok does not exists] ******************
ok: [localhost]

PLAY RECAP ******************************************************
localhost                  : ok=2    changed=1    unreachable=0    failed=0
```

As you can see, all tasks have been executed except the one with the `file_present` tag.

# Managing exceptions

There are many cases, where for one reason or another, you want your playbook and roles to carry on in the case one or more tasks fail. A typical example of this could be that you want to check if software is installed or not. Let's see the following example to install Java. In the `roles/java/tasks/main.ymal` file, we are going to put the following code:

```
    - name: Verify if the current version of Java is installed
      command: rpm -q jdk1.8.0_91-1.8.0_91-fcs
      register: java
      ignore_errors: True
      changed_when: java|failed

    - name: Ensure that JavaSE is download
      uri:
         url:
'http://download.oracle.com/otn-pub/java/jdk/8u91-b14/jdk-8u91-linux-x64.rpm'
```

```
            method: GET
            HEADER_Cookie: 'gpw_e24=http%3A%2F%2Fwww.oracle.com%2F;
 oraclelicense=accept-securebackup-cookie'
            dest: /tmp
            creates: /tmp/jdk-8u91-linux-x64.rpm
        when: java|failed

      - name: Ensure JavaSE is installed
        dnf:
            name: /tmp/jdk-8u91-linux-x64.rpm
            state: present
        when: java|failed

      - name: Set alternatives for java
        alternatives:
            path: /usr/java/jdk1.8.0_91/jre/bin/java
            name: java
            link: /usr/bin/java
        when: java|failed

      - name: Set alternatives for javac
        alternatives:
            path: /usr/java/jdk1.8.0_91/bin/javac
            name: javac
            link: /usr/bin/javac
        when: java|failed

      - name: Set alternatives for javaws
        alternatives:
            path: /usr/java/jdk1.8.0_91/bin/javaws
            name: javaws
            link: /usr/bin/javaws
        when: java|failed
```

Before going forward with the other parts that are needed to execute this role, I'd like to spend some words on the various parts of this role task list, since there are many new things:

```
      - name: Verify if the current version of Java is installed
        command: rpm -q jdk1.8.0_91-1.8.0_91-fcs
        register: java
        ignore_errors: True
        changed_when: java|failed
```

*Debugging and Error Handling*

In this task, we execute an `rpm` command that could have two different outputs:

- Fail
- Return the complete name of the JDK package

Since we only want to check if the package exists or not and then to go forward, we register the output (*third* line) and ignore eventual failures (*fourth* line):

```
- name: Ensure that JavaSE is download
  uri:
    url: 'http://download.oracle.com/otn-pub/java/jdk/8u91-b14/jdk-8u91-linux-x64.rpm'
    method: GET
    HEADER_Cookie: 'gpw_e24=http%3A%2F%2Fwww.oracle.com%2F; oraclelicense=accept-securebackup-cookie'
    dest: /tmp
    creates: /tmp/jdk-8u91-linux-x64.rpm
  when: java|failed
```

In this part, we use the `uri` module that allows us to hit a remote URI with an HTTP request. This module is very nice since it allows you to use all HTTP methods as well as to customize HTTP headers. This makes this module very flexible. Since in the last line we have `when: java|failed`, this will only be executed if Java is not installed:

```
- name: Ensure JavaSE is installed
  dnf:
    name: /tmp/jdk-8u91-linux-x64.rpm
    state: present
  when: java|failed
```

Here we use `dnf` to install the Java package. Since in the last line we have `when: java|failed`, this will only be executed if Java is not installed:

```
- name: Set alternatives for java
  alternatives:
    path: /usr/java/jdk1.8.0_91/jre/bin/java
    name: java
    link: /usr/bin/java
  when: java|failed

- name: Set alternatives for javac
  alternatives:
    path: /usr/java/jdk1.8.0_91/bin/javac
    name: javac
    link: /usr/bin/javac
  when: java|failed
```

```yaml
    - name: Set alternatives for javaws
      alternatives:
        path: /usr/java/jdk1.8.0_91/bin/javaws
        name: javaws
        link: /usr/bin/javaws
      when: java|failed
```

Here we are going to set new alternatives, in case we are installing Java. `alternatives` is an Ansible module that allows us to manage the configuration of the Linux `alternatives` program. This program is often used to manage which version of a program should be run by default in case you have multiple versions installed by default.

After we create the role, we will need the `hosts` file containing the host machine, in my case:

```
j01.fale.io
```

And a playbook to apply the role, placed in `playbooks/hosts/j01.fale.io.yaml` and with the following content:

```yaml
- hosts: j01.fale.io
  user: root
  roles:
    - java
```

We can now execute it with the following:

**ansible-playbook playbooks/hosts/j01.fale.io.yaml**

We will get the following result:

```
PLAY [j01.fale.io] *********************************************

TASK [setup] ***************************************************
ok: [j01.fale.io]

TASK [java : Verify if the current version of Java is installed] *
fatal: [j01.fale.io]: FAILED! => {"changed": true, "cmd": ["rpm", "-q", "jdk1.8.0_91-1.8.0_91-fcs"],         "delta": "0:00:00.009788", "end": "2016-09-27 11:04:56.185618", "failed": true, "rc": 1, "start":
"2016-    09-27 11:04:56.175830", "stderr": ``, "stdout": "package jdk1.8.0_91-1.8.0_91-fcs is not     installed", "stdout_lines":
["package jdk1.8.0_91-1.8.0_91-fcs is not installed"], "warnings":
    ["Consider using yum, dnf or zypper module rather than running rpm"]}
    ...ignoring

TASK [java : Ensure that JavaSE is download] ********************
changed: [j01.fale.io]
```

```
TASK [java : Ensure JavaSE is installed] *************************
changed: [j01.fale.io]

TASK [java : Set alternatives for java] **************************
ok: [j01.fale.io]

TASK [java : Set alternatives for javac] *************************
ok: [j01.fale.io]

TASK [java : Set alternatives for javaws] ************************
ok: [j01.fale.io]

PLAY RECAP *******************************************************
j01.fale.io              : ok=7    changed=2    unreachable=0    failed=0
```

As you can see, the installation check failed since Java was not installed on the machine, and for this reason all other tasks have been executed as expected.

# Trigger failure

There are cases when you want to trigger a failure directly. This can happen for multiple reasons, even if there are disadvantages doing so, since when you trigger the failure, the playbook will be brutally interrupted and this could leave your machine in an inconsistent state if you are not careful. One case where I have seen it work very well, is when you are running a non-idempotent playbook (for instance building of a newer version of an application) and you need a variable (for instance: the version/branch to deploy) set. In this case, you can check that the expected variable is correctly configured before starting to run the operations to ensure that everything will work as expected later on.

Let's put the following code in `playbooks/maven_build.yaml`:

```
- hosts: j01.fale.io
  tasks:
  - name: Ensure the tag variable is properly set
    fail: 'The version needs to be defined. To do so, please add: --extra-vars                         "version=$[TAG/BRANCH]"'
    when: version is not defined
  - name: Get last Project version
    git:
      repo: https://github.com/org/project.git
      dest: "/tmp"
      version: '{{ version }}'
  - name: Maven clean install
    shell: "cd /tmp/project && mvn clean install"
```

As you can see, we expect the user to add `--extra-vars "version=$[TAG/BRANCH]"` in the script to call the command. We could have put a branch to use by default but this is too risky because the user may lose focus and forget to add the right branch name themselves, which would lead to compiling (and deploying) the wrong version of the application. The `fail` module also allows us to specify a message that will be displayed to the user.

I think that the `fail` task is far more useful in playbooks that are run manually since when a playbook is automatically run, managing the exception is often better than failing.

# Summary

In this chapter, we have seen how to debug Ansible playbooks using multiple techniques. Then we moved to the management of failures and lastly we saw how to trigger failures intentionally.

In the next chapter, we will discuss multi-tier environments as well as deployment methodologies.

# 9
# Complex Environments

So far, we've seen how you can develop playbooks and test them. The final aspect is how to release playbooks into production. In most cases, you will have multiple environments to deal with before the playbook is released into production. This is similar to software that your developers have written. Many companies have multiple environments and usually your playbook will follow these steps:

- Development environment
- Testing environment
- Staging environment
- Production

Some companies name these environments in different ways, and some companies have additional environments such as certification where all software has to be certified before it can go to production.

When you write your playbooks and set up roles, we strongly recommend that you keep in mind the notion of the environments right from the start. It might be worthwhile to talk to your software and operations teams to figure out exactly how many environments your setup has to cater to.

## Code based on the Git branch

Let's assume you have four environments to take care of, which are as follows:

- Development
- Testing
- Stage
- Production

In the Git branch-based method, you will have one environment per branch. You will always make changes to **Development** first, and then promote those changes to **Testing** (merge or cherry-pick, and tag commits in Git), **Stage**, and **Production**. In this approach, you will hold one single inventory file, one set of variable files, and finally, a bunch of folders dedicated to roles and playbooks per branch.

## A single stable branch with multiple folders

In this approach, you will always maintain the dev and master branches. The initial code is committed to the dev branch, and once stable, you will promote it to the master branch. The same roles and playbooks that exist in the master branch will run across all environments. On the other hand, you will have separate folders for each of your environments. Let's look at an example. We'll show how you can have a separate configuration and an inventory for two environments: stage and production. You can extend it for your scenario to fit all the environments you use. Let's first look at the playbook in `playbooks/variables.yaml` that will run across these multiple environments and has the following content:

```
- hosts: web
  user: root
  tasks:
  - name: Print environment name
    debug:
      var: env
  - name: Print db server url
    debug:
      var: db_url
  - name: Print domain url
    debug:
```

```
      var: domain
- hosts: db
  user: root
  tasks:
  - name: Print environment name
    debug:
      var: env
  - name: Print database username
    debug:
      var: db_user
  - name: Print database password
    debug:
      var: db_pass
```

As you can see, there are two sets of tasks in this plays:

- Tasks that run against DB servers
- Tasks that run against web servers

There is also an extra task to print the environment name that is common to all servers in a particular environment. We will also have two different inventory files.

The first one will be called `inventory/production` with the following content:

```
[web]
ws01.fale.io
ws02.fale.io

[db]
db01.fale.io

[production:children]
db
web
```

The second one will be called `inventory/staging` with the following content:

```
[web]
ws01.stage.fale.io
ws02.stage.fale.io

[db]
db01.stage.fale.io

[staging:children]
db
web
```

## Complex Environments

As you can see, we have two machines for the `web` section and one for the `db` in each environment. Further, we have a different set of machines for stage and production environments. The additional section, `[ENVIRONMENT:children]`, allows you to create a group of groups. This would mean that any variables that are defined in the `ENVIRONMENT` section will apply to both the `db` and `web` groups, unless they're overridden in the individual sections, respectively. The next interesting part would be to look at variable values for each of the environments and see how they are separated out in each environment.

Let's start with the variables that will be the same for all our environments, located in `inventory/group_vars/all`:

```
db_user: mysqluser
```

The only variable that is the same for both our environments is the `db_user`.

We can now look at the production-specific variables, located in `inventory/group_vars/production`:

```
env: production
domain: fale.io
db_url: db.fale.io
db_pass: this_is_a_safe_password
```

If we now look at the stage-specific variables located in `inventory/group_vars/staging`, we will find the same variables we had in the production one, but with different values:

```
env: staging
domain: stage.fale.io
db_url: db.stage.fale.io
db_pass: this_is_an_unsafe_password
```

We can now validate that we receive the expected results. First we are going to run against the staging environment:

```
ansible-playbook -i staging playbooks/variables.yaml
```

And we should receive an output similar to the following:

```
PLAY [web] ************************************************


TASK [setup] ************************************************
ok: [ws02.stage.fale.io]
ok: [ws01.stage.fale.io]
```

```
TASK [Print environment name] *************************************
ok: [ws01.stage.fale.io] => {
    "env": "staging"
}
ok: [ws02.stage.fale.io] => {
    "env": "staging"
}


TASK [Print db server url] ****************************************
ok: [ws01.stage.fale.io] => {
    "db_url": "db.stage.fale.io"
}
ok: [ws02.stage.fale.io] => {
    "db_url": "db.stage.fale.io"
}


TASK [Print domain url] *******************************************
ok: [ws01.stage.fale.io] => {
    "domain": "stage.fale.io"
}
ok: [ws02.stage.fale.io] => {
    "domain": "stage.fale.io"
}


PLAY [db] *********************************************************


TASK [setup] ******************************************************
ok: [db01.stage.fale.io]


TASK [Print environment name] *************************************
ok: [db01.stage.fale.io] => {
    "env": "staging"
}


TASK [Print database username] ************************************
ok: [db01.stage.fale.io] => {
    "db_user": "mysqluser"
}


TASK [Print database password] ************************************
ok: [db01.stage.fale.io] => {
```

```
        "db_pass": "this_is_an_unsafe_password"
}


PLAY RECAP *********************************************************
db01.stage.fale.io: ok=4      changed=0     unreachable=0    failed=0
ws01.stage.fale.io: ok=4      changed=0     unreachable=0    failed=0
ws02.stage.fale.io: ok=4      changed=0     unreachable=0    failed=0
```

We can now run against the production environment:

```
ansible-playbook -i production playbooks/variables.yaml
```

We will receive the following result:

```
PLAY [web] *********************************************************

TASK [setup] *******************************************************
ok: [ws02.fale.io]
ok: [ws01.fale.io]

TASK [Print environment name] **************************************
ok: [ws01.fale.io] => {
    "env": "production"
}
ok: [ws02.fale.io] => {
    "env": "production"
}

TASK [Print db server url] *****************************************
ok: [ws01.fale.io] => {
    "db_url": "db.fale.io"
}
ok: [ws02.fale.io] => {
    "db_url": "db.fale.io"
}

TASK [Print domain url] ********************************************
ok: [ws01.fale.io] => {
    "domain": "fale.io"
}
ok: [ws02.fale.io] => {
    "domain": "fale.io"
}

PLAY [db] **********************************************************

TASK [setup] *******************************************************
```

[ 202 ]

```
ok: [db01.fale.io]

TASK [Print environment name] ***********************************
ok: [db01.fale.io] => {
    "env": "production"
}

TASK [Print database username] **********************************
ok: [db01.fale.io] => {
    "db_user": "mysqluser"
}

TASK [Parint database password] *********************************
ok: [db01.fale.io] => {
    "db_pass": "this_is_a_safe_password"
}

PLAY RECAP ******************************************************
db01.fale.io               : ok=4    changed=0    unreachable=0    failed=0
ws01.fale.io               : ok=4    changed=0    unreachable=0    failed=0
ws02.fale.io               : ok=4    changed=0    unreachable=0    failed=0
```

You can see that the Ansible run picked up all the relevant variables defined for the staging environment.

If you're using this approach to gain a stable master branch for multiple environments, it's best to use an amalgamation of environment-specific directories, group_vars, and inventory groups to tackle the scenario.

# Software distribution strategy

Deploying applications is probably one of the most complex tasks in the **Information and Communication Technology** (**ICT**) field. This is mainly caused by the fact that it often requires changing the state of the majority of machines that are somehow part of that application. In fact, often you find yourself having to change the state of load balancers, distribution servers, application servers, and database servers all at the same time during a deployment. New technologies, like containers, are trying to make those operations simpler, but often is not easy or possible to just move a legacy application to a container.

What we are now going to see are the various software distribution strategies and how Ansible can help with each one.

## Copying files from the local machine

This is probably the oldest strategy to distribute software. The idea is to have the files on the local machine (often used to develop the code) and as soon as the change is made, a copy of the file is put on the server (usually via FTP). This way of deploying code was often used for web development, where the code (usually in PHP) does not need any compilation.

This distribution strategy should be avoided due to its multiple problems:

- Very hard to rollback
- Impossible to track changes to the various deployments
- No deployment history
- Easy to make errors during the deployment

Although this distribution strategy can be very easily automated with Ansible, I strongly suggest you move immediately to a different strategy that allows you to have a safer distribution strategy.

## Revision control system with branches

Many companies are using this technique to distribute their software, mainly for uncompiled software. The idea behind this technique is to set up your server to use a local copy of your code repository. With SVN this was possible but not very easy to manage properly, while Git allowed a simplification of this technique, making it very popular.

This technique has many advantages over the one we have just seen, the main ones are:

- Easy rollbacks
- Very easy to obtain the history of changes
- Very easy deployments (mainly if Git is used)

On the other hand, this technique, still has multiple disadvantages:

- No deployment history
- Hard for compiled software
- Possible security problems

I'd like to discuss the possible security problems you can encounter with this technique a little bit more. What can be very tempting, is to download your Git repository directly in the folder that you use to distribute the content, so if it's a web server, the /var/www/ folder. This has obvious advantages since to deploy you'll only need to perform a git pull. The disadvantage is that Git will create the /var/www/.git folder which will contain your entire Git repository (history included) and, if not properly protected, will be freely downloadable by anyone.

About 1% of Alexa's top 1 million websites have the Git folder publicly accessible, so be very careful if you want to use this distribution strategy.

## Revision control system with tags

Another way of using revision control systems that is a little bit more complex but have some advantages, is leveraging the tagging system. This method requires to tag every time a new deployment has to be done and then checkout the specific tag on the server.

This has all the advantages of the previous method, with the addition of the deployment history. The compiled software problem and possible security problems are the same as in the previous method.

# RPM packages

A very common way to deploy software (mainly for compiled applications, but also advantageous for non-compiled applications) is using some kind of packaging system. Some languages, like Java, have an included system (the WAR, in Java case), but there are also packaging systems that can be used for any kind of applications, such as RPM. The disadvantage of these systems is that they are a little bit more complex than the previous methods, but those systems can grant a higher level of security as well as versioning. Also, these systems are easily injectable in a CI/CD pipeline, so the real complexity is much lower than what it could seem at first sight, since the CI/CD pipeline will take care of the building itself.

# Preparing the environment

To see how we can deploy the code in the various ways we talked about in the previous pages, we will need an environment, and obviously we are going to create it using Ansible. First of all, to ensure that our roles are properly loaded, we need the `ansible.cfg` file with the following content:

```
[defaults]
roles_path = roles
```

Then we need the `playbooks/firstrun.yaml` to ensure that we can configure our machines with a basic configuration, with the following content:

```
- hosts: all
  user: root
  tasks:
  - name: Ensure ansible user exists
    user:
      name: ansible
      state: present
      comment: Ansible
  - name: Ensure ansible user accepts the SSH key
    authorized_key:
      user: ansible
      key: https://github.com/fale.keys
      state: present
  - name: Ensure the ansible user is sudoer with no password required
    lineinfile:
      dest: /etc/sudoers
      state: present
      regexp: '^ansible ALL\='
      line: 'ansible ALL=(ALL) NOPASSWD:ALL'
```

```
      validate: 'visudo -cf %s'
```

The `playbooks/groups/web.yaml` will also need to be created to allow us to properly bootstrap our web servers:

```
- hosts: web
  user: ansible
  roles:
  - common
  - webserver
```

As you can imagine from the previous file content, we will need to create the roles: `common` and `webserver` which are very similar to the ones we created in Chapter 4, *Handling Complex Deployment*. We start with the `roles/common/tasks/main.yaml` file with the following content:

```
- name: Ensure EPEL is enabled
  yum:
    name: epel-release
    state: present
  become: True
- name: Ensure needed packages are present
  yum:
    name: '{{ item }}'
    state: present
  become: True
  with_items:
  - libsemanage-python
  - libselinux-python
  - ntp
  - firewalld
- name: Ensure we have last version of every package
  yum:
    name: "*"
    state: latest
  become: True
- name: Ensure the timezone is set to UTC
  file:
    src: /usr/share/zoneinfo/GMT
    dest: /etc/localtime
    state: link
  become: True
- name: Ensure the NTP service is running and enabled
  service:
    name: ntpd
    state: started
    enabled: True
```

```yaml
      become: True
    - name: Ensure FirewallD is running
      service:
        name: firewalld
        state: started
        enabled: True
      become: True
    - name: Ensure SSH can pass the firewall
      firewalld:
        service: ssh
        state: enabled
        permanent: True
        immediate: True
      become: True
    - name: Ensure the MOTD file is present and updated
      template:
        src: motd
        dest: /etc/motd
        owner: root
        group: root
        mode: 0644
      become: True
    - name: Ensure the hostname is the same of the inventory
      hostname:
        name: "{{ inventory_hostname }}"
      become: True
```

It's `motd` template is in `roles/common/templates/motd`:

```
                This system is managed by Ansible
    Any change done on this system could be overwritten by Ansible

    OS: {{ ansible_distribution }} {{ ansible_distribution_version }}
    Hostname: {{ inventory_hostname }}
    eth0 address: {{ ansible_eth0.ipv4.address }}

                All connections are monitored and recorded
        Disconnect IMMEDIATELY if you are not an authorized user
```

We can now move to the `webserver` role, more specifically to the `roles/webserver/tasks/main.yaml` file:

```yaml
    - name: Ensure the HTTPd package is installed
      yum:
        name: httpd
        state: present
      become: True
    - name: Ensure the PHP is installed
```

```yaml
      yum:
        name: '{{ item }}'
        state: present
      become: True
      with_items:
       - git
       - php
    - name: Ensure the HTTPd service is enabled and running
      service:
        name: httpd
        state: started
        enabled: True
      become: True
    - name: Ensure HTTP can pass the firewall
      firewalld:
        service: http
        state: enabled
        permanent: True
        immediate: True
      become: True
    - name: Ensure HTTPd configuration is updated
      copy:
        src: website.conf
        dest: /etc/httpd/conf.d
      become: True
      notify: Restart HTTPd
```

We also need to create the handler in `roles/webserver/handlers/main.yaml` with the content:

```yaml
    - name: Restart HTTPd
      service:
        name: httpd
        state: restarted
      become: True
```

Lastly, we need to touch the `roles/webserver/files/website.conf` file, leaving it empty for now, but it needs to exist.

# Complex Environments

We can now provision a couple of CentOS machines (I provisioned `ws01.fale.io` and `ws02.fale.io`) and ensure that the inventory is right. We can also run the `firstrun.yaml` playbook to ensure that the Ansible user is present and properly configured:

```
ansible-playbook -i inventory/production playbooks/firstrun.yaml
```

The output you should receive is the following:

```
PLAY [localhost] ************************************************

PLAY [all] ******************************************************

TASK [setup] ****************************************************
ok: [ws01.fale.io]
ok: [ws02.fale.io]

TASK [Ensure ansible user exists] *******************************
changed: [ws01.fale.io]
changed: [ws02.fale.io]

TASK [Ensure ansible user accepts the SSH key] ******************
changed: [ws01.fale.io]
changed: [ws02.fale.io]

TASK [Ensure the ansible user is sudoer with no password required]
changed: [ws01.fale.io]
changed: [ws02.fale.io]

PLAY RECAP ******************************************************
ws01.fale.io      : ok=4    changed=3    unreachable=0    failed=0
ws02.fale.io      : ok=4    changed=3    unreachable=0    failed=0
```

We can now configure those machines running their group playbook:

```
ansible-playbook -i inventory/production playbooks/groups/web.yaml
```

We will receive the following output:

```
PLAY [web] ******************************************************

TASK [setup] ****************************************************
ok: [ws01.fale.io]
ok: [ws02.fale.io]
....

PLAY RECAP ******************************************************
ws01.fale.io      : ok=20   changed=14   unreachable=0    failed=0
```

```
        ws02.fale.io          : ok=20    changed=14    unreachable=0    failed=0
```

We can now point our browser to our nodes on port `80` to check that the HTTPd page is displayed as expected.

# Deploying a web app with revision control systems

For this example, we are going to deploy a simple PHP application that will be composed of only a single PHP page. The source is available on the following repository: https://github.com/Fale/demo-php-app.

To deploy it, we will need the following code placed in `playbooks/manual/rcs_deploy.yaml`:

```
- hosts: web
  user: ansible
  tasks:
  - name: Install or update website
    git:
      repo: https://github.com/Fale/demo-php-app.git
      dest: /var/www/application
    become: True
```

We can now run the **deployer** with the following command:

```
ansible-playbook -i inventory/production playbooks/manual/rcs_deploy.yaml
```

This is the expected result:

```
PLAY [web] ************************************************************

TASK [setup] **********************************************************
ok: [ws01.fale.io]
ok: [ws02.fale.io]
....

PLAY RECAP ************************************************************
ws01.fale.io           : ok=2     changed=1     unreachable=0    failed=0
ws02.fale.io           : ok=2     changed=1     unreachable=0    failed=0
```

## Complex Environments

At the moment, our application is not yet reachable since we have no HTTPd rule for that folder. To achieve this, we will need to change the `roles/webserver/files/website.conf` file with the following content:

```
<VirtualHost *:80>
    ServerName app.fale.io
    DocumentRoot /var/www/application
    <Directory /var/www/application>
        Options None
    </Directory>
    <DirectoryMatch ".git*">
        Require all denied
    </DirectoryMatch>
</VirtualHost>
```

As you can see, we are just displaying this application to the users reaching our server with the `app.fale.io` URL and not to everyone. This will ensure that all your users will have a consistent experience. Also, you can see that we are blocking all access to the `.git` folder (and all its content). This is needed for security reasons we mentioned earlier in the chapter.

We can now re-run the web playbook to ensure that our HTTPd configuration gets propagated with:

```
ansible-playbook -i inventory/production playbooks/groups/web.yaml
```

This is the result we are going to receive:

```
PLAY [web] ************************************************************

TASK [setup] **********************************************************
ok: [ws01.fale.io]
ok: [ws02.fale.io]

TASK [common : Ensure EPEL is enabled] ****************************
ok: [ws01.fale.io]
ok: [ws02.fale.io]

TASK [common : Ensure libselinux-python is present] **************
ok: [ws01.fale.io]
ok: [ws02.fale.io]

TASK [common : Ensure libsemanage-python is present] *************
ok: [ws01.fale.io]
ok: [ws02.fale.io]

TASK [common : Ensure we have last version of every package] *****
ok: [ws01.fale.io]
```

```
ok: [ws02.fale.io]

TASK [common : Ensure NTP is installed] **************************
ok: [ws01.fale.io]
ok: [ws02.fale.io]

TASK [common : Ensure the timezone is set to UTC] ****************
ok: [ws01.fale.io]
ok: [ws02.fale.io]

TASK [common : Ensure the NTP service is running and enabled] ****
ok: [ws01.fale.io]
ok: [ws02.fale.io]

TASK [common : Ensure FirewallD is installed] ********************
ok: [ws01.fale.io]
ok: [ws02.fale.io]

TASK [common : Ensure FirewallD is running] **********************
ok: [ws01.fale.io]
ok: [ws02.fale.io]

TASK [common : Ensure SSH can pass the firewall] *****************
ok: [ws01.fale.io]
ok: [ws02.fale.io]

TASK [common : Ensure the MOTD file is present and updated] ******
ok: [ws01.fale.io]
ok: [ws02.fale.io]

TASK [common : Ensure the hostname is the same of the inventory] *
ok: [ws01.fale.io]
ok: [ws02.fale.io]

TASK [webserver : Ensure the HTTPd package is installed] *********
ok: [ws01.fale.io]
ok: [ws02.fale.io]

TASK [webserver : Ensure the PHP is installed] *******************
ok: [ws01.fale.io]
ok: [ws02.fale.io]

TASK [webserver : Ensure git is installed] ***********************
ok: [ws01.fale.io]
ok: [ws02.fale.io]

TASK [webserver : Ensure the HTTPd service is enabled and running]
ok: [ws01.fale.io]
```

```
                ok: [ws02.fale.io]

                TASK [webserver : Ensure HTTP can pass the firewall] *************
                ok: [ws01.fale.io]
                ok: [ws02.fale.io]

                TASK [webserver : Ensure HTTPd configuration is updated] *********
                changed: [ws01.fale.io]
                changed: [ws02.fale.io]

                RUNNING HANDLER [webserver : Restart HTTPd] *********************
                changed: [ws01.fale.io]
                changed: [ws02.fale.io]

                PLAY RECAP *****************************************************
                ws01.fale.io         : ok=20    changed=2    unreachable=0    failed=0
                ws02.fale.io         : ok=20    changed=2    unreachable=0    failed=0
```

You can now check and see that everything works properly.

# Deploying a web app with RPM packages

In order to deploy an RPM package, we will need to create it in the first place. To do so, the first thing we need is a Spec file.

## Creating a Spec file

The first thing to do is to create a **Specifics** (**Spec**) file, which is a recipe for instructing `rpmbuild` on how to actually create the RPM package. We are going to locate the Spec file in `spec/demo-php-app.spec` and put the following content into it:

```
%define debug_package %{nil}
%global commit0 b49f595e023e07a8345f47a3ad62a6f50f03121e
%global shortcommit0 %(c=%{commit0}; echo ${c:0:7})

Name:           demo-php-app
Version:        0
Release:        1%{?dist}
Summary:        Demo PHP application

License:        PD
URL:            https://github.com/Fale/demo-php-app
Source0:        %{url}/archive/%{commit0}.tar.gz#/%{name}-%{shortcommit0}.tar.gz
```

```
%description
This is a demo PHP application in RPM format

%prep
%autosetup -n %{name}-%{commit0}

%build

%install
mkdir -p %{buildroot}/var/www/application
ls -alh
cp index.php %{buildroot}/var/www/application

%files
%dir /var/www/application
/var/www/application/index.php

%changelog
* Tue Oct 04 2016 Fabio Alessandro Locati - 0.1
- Initial packaging
```

Let's see what the various parts do and mean before moving forward:

```
%define debug_package %{nil}
%global commit0 b49f595e023e07a8345f47a3ad62a6f50f03121e
%global shortcommit0 %(c=%{commit0}; echo ${c:0:7})
```

These first three lines are variables declarations.

The first one will disable the generation of a debug package. By default, `rpmbuild` will create a debug package every time and include all debugging symbols, but in this case, we don't have any debugging symbols since we are not making any compilation.

The second puts the **hash** of the commit in the variable `commit0`. The third one calculates the value of `shortcommit0`, that is calculated as the first eight characters of the `commit0` string:

```
Name:       demo-php-app
Version:    0
Release:    1%{?dist}
Summary:    Demo PHP application

License:    PD
URL:        https://github.com/Fale/demo-php-app
Source0:    %{url}/archive/%{commit0}.tar.gz#/%{name}-%{shortcommit0}.tar.gz
```

## Complex Environments

In the first line, we declare the name, version, release number, and summary. The difference between version and release, is that the version is the upstream version, while the release is the Spec version for that upstream release.

The license is the source license, not the Spec license. The URL is used to track the upstream website. The `source0` field is used by `rpmbuild` to know how the source file is called (in case more than one file is present, we can user `source1`, `source2`, and so on). Also, if the source fields are valid URI, we can use `spectool` to download them automatically.

```
%description
This is a demo PHP application in RPM format
```

This is the `description` of the software packaged in RPM package.

```
%prep
%autosetup -n %{name}-%{commit0}
```

The `prep` phase is the one where the source(s) get uncompressed and eventual patch(es) and applied. The `%autosetup` will uncompress the first source, as well as apply all patches. In this part, you can also perform other operations that need to be executed before the building phase and have the goal to prepare the environment for the build phase:

```
%build
```

Here we would put all actions of the `build` phase. In our case, our sources do not need to be compiled and therefore it is empty:

```
%install
mkdir -p %{buildroot}/var/www/application
ls -alh
cp index.php %{buildroot}/var/www/application
```

In the `install` phase, we put the files in the folder `%{buildroot}` that will mimic the target filesystem.

```
%files
%dir /var/www/application
/var/www/application/index.php
```

The `files` section is needed to declare which files are to be put in the package.

```
%changelog
* Tue Oct 04 2016 Fabio Alessandro Locati - 0.1
- Initial packaging
```

The `changelog` is needed to track who released a new version when and with which changes.

Now that we have the Spec file, we need to build it. To do so, we could use a production machine, but this would increase the attack surface to that machine, so it's better to avoid one. There are multiple ways to build your RPM software. The four main ways are:

- Manually
- Automate the manual way with Ansible
- Jenkins
- Koji

Let's look at the differences very briefly.

## Building RPMs manually

The simplest way to build an RPM package is doing so in a manual way.

The big advantage is that you need very few and easy to install packages and for this reason many people that are starting with RPM, start from here. The disadvantage is that the process will be manual, and therefore human errors can spoil the result and the procedure is not easy to audit.

To build RPM packages, you will need a Fedora or an EL (Red Hat Enterprise Linux, CentOS, Scientific Linux, Oracle Enterprise Linux) system. If you are using Fedora, you will need to execute the following command to install all needed software:

```
sudo dnf install -y fedora-packager
```

If you are running an EL system, the command you'll need to execute is:

```
sudo yum install -y mock rpm-build spectool
```

In either case, you'll need to add the user you'll use to the `mock` group, to do so, you need to execute:

```
sudo usermod -a -G mock [yourusername]
```

Linux loads the users at login, so to apply a group change, you need to restart your session.

At this point, we can copy the Spec file in folder (usually $HOME is a good one) and perform the following actions:

```
mkdir -p ~/rpmbuild/SOURCES
```

This will create the $HOME/rpmbuild/SOURCES folder that is needed in the process. The -p option will automatically create all folders in the path that are eventually missing.

```
spectool -R -g demo-php-app.spec
```

We used spectool to download the source file and place it in the appropriate directory. The spectool will automatically get the URL from the Spec file so that we don't have to remember it.

We now need to create an src.rpm file, to do so we can use rpmbuild:

```
rpmbuild -bs demo-php-app.spec
```

This command will output something like:

```
Wrote: /home/fale/rpmbuild/SRPMS/demo-php-app-0-1.fc24.src.rpm
```

Some small differences in the name could be present, for instance you will probably have a different $HOME folder and you could have something other than fc24, if you are using something different than Fedora 24 to build the package. At this point, we can create the binary file with:

```
mock -r epel-7-x86_64 /home/fale/rpmbuild/SRPMS/demo-php-app-0-1.fc24.src.rpm
```

Mock allows us to build RPM packages in a clean environment and also, thanks to the -r option, it allows us to build for different versions of Fedora, EL, and Mageia. This command will give you a very long output, that I'll not report here, but in the last few lines there is useful information. If everything built properly, this is the last few lines you should see:

```
Wrote: /builddir/build/RPMS/demo-php-app-0-1.el7.centos.x86_64.rpm
Executing(%clean): /bin/sh -e /var/tmp/rpm-tmp.d4vPhr
+ umask 022
+ cd /builddir/build/BUILD
+ cd demo-php-app-b49f595e023e07a8345f47a3ad62a6f50f03121e
+ /usr/bin/rm -rf /builddir/build/BUILDROOT/demo-php-app-0-1.el7.centos.x86_64
+ exit 0
Finish: rpmbuild demo-php-app-0-1.fc24.src.rpm
Finish: build phase for demo-php-app-0-1.fc24.src.rpm
```

```
        INFO: Done (/home/fale/rpmbuild/SRPMS/demo-php-app-0-1.fc24.src.rpm)
Config(epel-7-x86_64) 0 minutes 58 seconds
        INFO: Results and/or logs in: /var/lib/mock/epel-7-x86_64/result
        Finish: run
```

The second to last line contains the path where you can find the results. If you look in that folder, you should find the following files:

```
drwxrwsr-x. 2 fale mock 4.0K Oct 10 12:26 .
drwxrwsr-x. 4 root mock 4.0K Oct 10 12:25 ..
-rw-rw-r--. 1 fale mock 4.6K Oct 10 12:26 build.log
-rw-rw-r--. 1 fale mock 3.3K Oct 10 12:26 demo-php-
app-0-1.el7.centos.src.rpm
-rw-rw-r--. 1 fale mock 3.1K Oct 10 12:26 demo-php-
app-0-1.el7.centos.x86_64.rpm
-rw-rw-r--. 1 fale mock 184K Oct 10 12:26 root.log
-rw-rw-r--. 1 fale mock  792 Oct 10 12:26 state.log
```

The three log files are very useful in case of problems during the compilation. The `src.rpm` file will be a copy of the `src.rpm` file we created with the first command, while the `x86_64.rpm` file is the one mock created and the one we will need to install on our machines.

## Building RPMs with Ansible

Since doing all those steps manually can be long, boring, and error prone, we can automatize them with Ansible. The resulting playbook will probably not be the cleanest one, but will be able to execute all operations in a repeatable way.

For this reason, we are going to build a new machine from scratch. I'll call this machine `builder01.fale.io` and we are also going to change the inventory/production file to match this change:

```
[web]
ws01.fale.io
ws02.fale.io

[db]
db01.fale.io

[builders]
builder01.fale.io

[production:children]
db
```

```
    web
    builders
```

Before diving in the `builders` role, we will need to do a couple of changes to the `webserver` roles to enable a new repository. The first is adding a task in `roles/webserver/tasks/main.yaml` at the end of the file with the following code:

```
- name: Install our private repository
  copy:
    src: privaterepo.repo
    dest: /etc/yum.repos.d/privaterepo.repo
  become: True
```

And the second change is actually creating the `roles/webserver/files/privaterepo.repo` file with the following content:

```
[privaterepo]
name=Private repo that will keep our apps packages
baseurl=http://repo.fale.io/
skip_if_unavailable=True
gpgcheck=0
enabled=1
enabled_metadata=1
```

We can now execute the `webserver` group playbook to make the changes effective with:

```
ansible-playbook -i inventory/production playbooks/groups/web.yaml
```

And the following output should appear:

```
PLAY [web] ************************************************************

TASK [setup] **********************************************************
ok: [ws01.fale.io]
ok: [ws02.fale.io]
....

PLAY RECAP ************************************************************
ws01.fale.io        : ok=20    changed=1    unreachable=0    failed=0
ws02.fale.io        : ok=20    changed=1    unreachable=0    failed=0
```

As expected, the only change has been the deployment of our newly generated repository file.

We also need to create a role for `builders` with a `tasks` file located in `roles/builder/tasks/main.yaml` with the following content:

```yaml
- name: Ensure needed packages are present
  yum:
    name: '{{ item }}'
    state: present
  become: True
  with_items:
  - mock
  - rpm-build
  - spectool
  - createrepo
  - httpd

- name: Ensure the user ansible is in the mock group
  user:
    name: ansible
    groups: mock
    append: True
  become: True

- name: Ensure the /var/www/repo folder is present
  file:
    name: /var/www/repo
    state: directory
    group: ansible
    owner: ansible
    mode: 0755
  become: True

- name: Ensure the HTTPd zone for the repo is present
  copy:
    src: repo.conf
    dest: /etc/httpd/conf.d/repo.conf
  become: True
  notify: Restart HTTPd

- name: Ensure the HTTPd service is enabled and running
  service:
    name: httpd
    state: started
    enabled: True
  become: True

- name: Ensure HTTP can pass the firewall
  firewalld:
    service: http
```

```
      state: enabled
      permanent: True
      immediate: True
    become: True
```

Also, as part of the `builders` role, we need the `roles/builder/handlers/main.yaml` handler file with the following content:

```
- name: Restart HTTPd
  service:
    name: httpd
    state: restarted
  become: True
```

As you can guess from the tasks file, we will also need the `roles/builder/files/repo.conf` file with the following content:

```
<VirtualHost *:80>
    ServerName repo.fale.io
    DocumentRoot /var/www/repo
    <Directory /var/www/repo>
        Options Indexes FollowSymLinks
    </Directory>
</VirtualHost>
```

We also need a new `group` playbook in `playbooks/groups/builders.yaml` with the following content:

```
- hosts: builders
  user: ansible
  roles:
  - common
  - builder
```

We can now execute the `firstrun` playbook against it with:

**ansible-playbook -i inventory/production playbooks/firstrun.yaml -lbuilder01.fale.io**

And we will receive the following output:

```
PLAY [all] *************************************************

TASK [setup] ***********************************************
ok: [builder01.fale.io]

TASK [Ensure ansible user exists] **************************
changed: [builder01.fale.io]

TASK [Ensure ansible user accepts the SSH key] *************
changed: [builder01.fale.io]

TASK [Ensure the ansible user is sudoer with no password required]
changed: [builder01.fale.io]

PLAY RECAP *************************************************
builder01.fale.io  : ok=4    changed=3    unreachable=0    failed=0
```

We can now move to create the host itself with:

```
ansible-playbook -i inventory/production playbooks/groups/builders.yaml
```

And we are expecting a result similar to:

```
PLAY [builders] ********************************************

TASK [setup] ***********************************************
ok: [builder01.fale.io]
....

PLAY RECAP *************************************************
builder01.fale.io  : ok=23   changed=5    unreachable=0    failed=0
```

Now that we have all the parts of the infrastructure ready, we can create the playbooks/manual/rpm_deploy.yaml with the following content:

```
- hosts: builders
  user: ansible
  tasks:
  - name: Copy Spec file to user folder
    copy:
      src: ../../spec/demo-php-app.spec
      dest: /home/ansible
  - name: Ensure rpmbuild exists
    file:
      name: ~/rpmbuild
      state: directory
```

# Complex Environments

```yaml
    - name: Ensure rpmbuild/SOURCES exists
      file:
        name: ~/rpmbuild/SOURCES
        state: directory
    - name: Download the sources
      command: spectool -R -g demo-php-app.spec
    - name: Ensure no SRPM files are present
      command: rm -f ~/rpmbuild/SRPMS/*
    - name: Build the SRPM file
      command: rpmbuild -bs demo-php-app.spec
    - name: Execute mock
      shell: mock ~/rpmbuild/SRPMS/*
    - name: Copy the arch binaries in the repo path
      shell: cp -f /var/lib/mock/epel-7-x86_64/result/*.x86_64.rpm /var/www/repo
    - name: Recreate the repo metadata
      command: createrepo --database /var/www/repo
- hosts: web
  user: ansible
  tasks:
    - name: Ensure last version of demo-php-app is present
      yum:
        state: latest
        update_cache: True
        disable_gpg_check: True
        name: demo-php-app
      become: True
```

As discussed, this playbook has a lot of commands and shells which are not very clean. Probably, in the future it will be possible to write a playbook with the same features but with modules. Most actions are the same as we discussed in the previous section. The new actions are toward the end, in fact in this case we copy the generated RPM file to a specific folder, we invoke `createrepo` to generate a repository in that folder, and then we force all web servers to update the generated package to the last version.

 To grant the security of your application, is important that the repository is only accessible internally and not publicly.

We can now run the playbook with:

```
ansible-playbook -i inventory/production playbooks/manual/rpm_deploy.yaml
```

And we expect a result like the following:

```
PLAY [builders] *********************************************

TASK [setup] ************************************************
ok: [builder01.fale.io]

TASK [Copy SPEC file to user folder] ************************
changed: [builder01.fale.io]

TASK [Ensure rpmbuild exists] *******************************
changed: [builder01.fale.io]

TASK [Ensure rpmbuild/SOURCES exists] ***********************
changed: [builder01.fale.io]

TASK [Download the sources] *********************************
changed: [builder01.fale.io]

TASK [Ensure no SRPM files are present] *********************
changed: [builder01.fale.io]

TASK [Build the SRPM file] **********************************
changed: [builder01.fale.io]

TASK [Execute mock] *****************************************
changed: [builder01.fale.io]

TASK [Copy the arch binaries in the repo path] **************
changed: [builder01.fale.io]

TASK [Recreate the repo metadata] ***************************
changed: [builder01.fale.io]

PLAY [web] **************************************************

TASK [setup] ************************************************
ok: [ws01.fale.io]
ok: [ws02.fale.io]

TASK [Update all packages] **********************************
changed: [ws01.fale.io]
changed: [ws02.fale.io]

PLAY RECAP **************************************************
builder01.fale.io  : ok=10    changed=9    unreachable=0    failed=0
ws01.fale.io       : ok=2     changed=1    unreachable=0    failed=0
ws02.fale.io       : ok=2     changed=1    unreachable=0    failed=0
```

# Building RPMs with CI/CD pipelines

Although this is not covered by this book, in more complex cases you may want to use a CI/CD pipeline to create and manage RPM packages. The two main pipelines are based on two different software: Jenkins and Koji.

The Koji software has been developed by the Fedora community and Red Hat. It is released under the terms of the LGPL 2.1 license. This is the pipeline that currently gets used by Fedora, CentOS, as well as many other companies and communities to create all their RPMs (both for official and testing-aka **scratch builds**-builds). Koji – by default is not triggered by commit, but needs to be called "manually" from a user (through web interface or CLI). Koji will automatically download the last version of the Spec Git, download the source from a side-cache (this is optional, but suggested) or from the original location, and trigger the mock build. Koji does support only mock due to the fact that is the only system that allows consistent and repeatable builds. Koji can store all output artifacts forever or for a limited amount of time, based on the configuration. This is to ensure a very high level of auditability.

Jenkins is one of the most used CI/CD managers and can also be used for RPM pipelines. The big disadvantage is that it needs to be configured from scratch with the consequence that more time is required, but this means it has more flexibility. Also, a big advantage of Jenkins is that many companies already have an instance of Jenkins, and this makes it easier to set up and maintain the infrastructure, since you can reuse an installation you already have, having to manage less systems overall.

# Building compiled software with RPM packaging

RPM packaging is very useful for non-binary applications and close to a necessity for binary applications. This is also true because the difference in complexity is pretty low between a non-binary and a binary case. In fact, the build and the installation will work in exactly the same way. The only thing that will change is the Spec file.

Let's see for example the Spec file needed to compile and package a simple Hello World! application written in C:

```
%global commit0 7c288b9d80a6ef525c0cca8a744b32e018eaa386
%global shortcommit0 %(c=%{commit0}; echo ${c:0:7})

Name:           hello-world
Version:        1.0
```

```
Release:          1%{?dist}
Summary:          Hello World example implemented in C

License:          GPLv3+
URL:              https://github.com/Fale/hello-world
Source0:          %{url}/archive/%{commit0}.tar.gz#/%{name}-%{shortcommit0}.tar.gz

BuildRequires:    gcc
BuildRequires:    make

%description
The description for our Hello World Example implemented in C

%prep
%autosetup -n %{name}-%{commit0}

%build
make %{?_smp_mflags}

%install
%make_install

%files
%license LICENSE
%{_bindir}/hello

%changelog
* Tue Oct 11 2016 Fabio Alessandro Locati - 1.0-1
- Initial packaging
```

As you can see, it's very similar to the one we saw for the PHP demo application. Let's see the differences.

```
%global commit0 7c288b9d80a6ef525c0cca8a744b32e018eaa386
%global shortcommit0 %(c=%{commit0}; echo ${c:0:7})
```

As you can see, we don't have the line to disable the debug package. Every time you package a compiled application, you should let `rpm` create the debug symbols package so that in case of crashes, it will be easier to debug and understand the problem.

```
Name:       hello-world
Version:    1.0
Release:    1%{?dist}
Summary:    Hello World example implemented in C

License:    GPLv3+
URL:        https://github.com/Fale/hello-world
```

```
Source0:          %{url}/archive/%{commit0}.tar.gz#/%{name}-
%{shortcommit0}.tar.gz
```

As you can see, the changes in this section are only due to the fact that the new package has a different name and URL, but are not linked to the fact that is a compliable application.

```
BuildRequires:    gcc
BuildRequires:    make
```

In the non-compiled application we did not need any packages present at build time, while in this case we will need the make and the gcc (compiler) applications. Different applications could require different tools and or libraries to be present on the system at build time.

```
%description
The description for our Hello World Example implemented in C

%prep
%autosetup -n %{name}-%{commit0}

%build
make %{?_smp_mflags}
```

The description is package-specific and is not influenced by the compilation of the package. In the same way, the %prep phase works.

In the %build phase we now have make %{?_smp_mflags}. This is needed to tell rpmbuild to actually run make to build our application. The _smp_mflags variable will include a set of parameters to optimize the compilation to be multi-thread.

```
%install
%make_install
```

During the %install phase, we will issue the %make_install command. This macro will call %make_install with a set of additional parameters to ensure that the **libraries** are located in the right folder, as well as the binaries and so forth.

```
%files
%license LICENSE
%{_bindir}/hello
```

In this case, we only need to place the `hello` binary that was located in the right folder of the `buildroot` during the `%install` phase as well as add the `LICENSE` file containing the license.

```
%changelog
* Tue Oct 11 2016 Fabio Alessandro Locati - 1.0-1
- Initial packaging
```

The `%changelog` is very similar to the other Spec file we saw, since it is not influenced by the involvement of a compilation.

After you completed this, you can place it in `spec/hello-world.spec` and tweak `playbooks/manual/rpm_deploy.yaml` saving it into `playbooks/manual/hello_deploy.yaml` with the following content:

```
- hosts: builders
  user: ansible
  tasks:
  - name: Copy Spec file to user folder
    copy:
      src: ../../spec/hello-world.spec
      dest: /home/ansible
  - name: Ensure rpmbuild exists
    file:
      name: ~/rpmbuild
      state: directory
  - name: Ensure rpmbuild/SOURCES exists
    file:
      name: ~/rpmbuild/SOURCES
      state: directory
  - name: Download the sources
    command: spectool -R -g hello-world.spec
  - name: Ensure no SRPM files are present
    command: rm -f ~/rpmbuild/SRPMS/*
  - name: Build the SRPM file
    command: rpmbuild -bs hello-world.spec
  - name: Execute mock
    shell: mock ~/rpmbuild/SRPMS/*
  - name: Copy the arch binaries in the repo path
    shell: cp -f /var/lib/mock/epel-7-x86_64/result/*.x86_64.rpm /var/www/repo
  - name: Recreate the repo metadata
    command: createrepo --database /var/www/repo
- hosts: web
  user: ansible
  tasks:
  - name: Ensure last version of hello-world is present
```

```yaml
    yum:
      state: latest
      update_cache: True
      disable_gpg_check: True
      name: hello-world
    become: True
```

As you can see, the only thing that we changes is that all references to `demo-php-app` got replaced with `hello-world`. Running it with:

```
ansible-playbook -i inventory/production playbooks/manual/hello_deploy.yaml
```

We are going to have the following result:

```
PLAY [builders] **********************************************

TASK [setup] *************************************************
ok: [builder01.fale.io]

TASK [Copy SPEC file to user folder] *************************
changed: [builder01.fale.io]

TASK [Ensure rpmbuild exists] ********************************
ok: [builder01.fale.io]

TASK [Ensure rpmbuild/SOURCES exists] ************************
ok: [builder01.fale.io]

TASK [Download the sources] **********************************
changed: [builder01.fale.io]

TASK [Ensure no SRPM files are present] **********************
changed: [builder01.fale.io]

TASK [Build the SRPM file] ***********************************
changed: [builder01.fale.io]

TASK [Execute mock] ******************************************
changed: [builder01.fale.io]

TASK [Copy the arch binaries in the repo path] ***************
changed: [builder01.fale.io]

TASK [Recreate the repo metadata] ****************************
changed: [builder01.fale.io]

PLAY [web] ***************************************************

TASK [setup] *************************************************
```

```
ok: [ws01.fale.io]
ok: [ws02.fale.io]

TASK [Ensure last version of hello-world is present] *************
changed: [ws01.fale.io]
changed: [ws02.fale.io]

PLAY RECAP *******************************************************
builder01.fale.io  : ok=10    changed=7    unreachable=0    failed=0
ws01.fale.io       : ok=2     changed=1    unreachable=0    failed=0
ws02.fale.io       : ok=2     changed=1    unreachable=0    failed=0
```

 You could eventually create a playbook that accepts the name of the package to build as a parameter, so that you don't need a different playbook for every package.

# Deployment strategies

We have seen how to distribute software in your environment, let's now speak about deployment strategies; that is how to upgrade your application without your service suffering from it.

There are three different problems you might incur during an update:

- Downtime during the update rollout
- The new version has problems
- The new version seems to work, until it fails

The first problem is known to every system administrator. During the update, you are probably going to restart some services, and for the time between the stop and the start of the service, your application will not be available on that machine. To avoid this also means that your application is not available at all; you will need to have at least some machines with the application available and a smart load balancer in front that will remove (and add them back when is the case) all nonfunctioning nodes.

The second problem can be prevented in multiple ways. The cleanest one would be testing in the CI/CD pipeline. In fact, those kinds of problems are pretty easy to find with simple tests. This can also be prevented with the methods we are going to see soon.

# Complex Environments

The third problem is by far the most complex. Many big down have been generated by these kinds of problems. Usually the problem is that the new version has some performance problems or memory leaks. Since the majority of deployments are done in the period of least load of the servers, as soon as the load increases, a performance problem or memory leak could kill your servers.

To be able to use those methods in a proper way, you have to be able to ensure that your software can accept rollbacks. There are cases where this is not possible (that is, a database table gets removed in an update) but should be avoided. We will not speak how to avoid it since is part of the development strategy, and is not related to Ansible.

## Canary deployment

The canary deployment is a technique that involves updating a small percentage of your machines (often 5%) to the new version and instruct the load balancers to send only an equivalent amount of traffic to it. This has several advantages:

- During the update, you never have less than 95% of the capacity
- If the new version completely fails, you lose the 5% of capacity
- Since the load-balancer divides the traffic between your new and old version, if the new version has problems, only 5% of your users will see the problem
- You only need to have 5% capacity more than your expected load

Canary deployment is able to prevent all three problems we mentioned with a very small overhead (5%) and with a low cost in case of rollback (5%). For those reasons, this technique is used a lot by huge companies; progressive rollout. Often to ensure a similar user experience to users that live close to each other, geography is used to choose if the user is going to hit the old or the new version.

When the test seems to be a success, the percentage can be increased progressively until 100% is reached.

It's possible to implement a canary deployment in multiple ways in Ansible. The way I suggest is the cleanest one; using the inventory files, more specifically, to have something like the following:

```
[web-main]
ws[00:94].fale.io

[web-canary]
ws[95:99].fale.io
```

```
[web:children]
web-main
web-canary
```

In this way, you can set all variables on the web group (the variables are going to be the same no matter the version, or at least they should be) but you can run a playbook easily against the canary group, the main group, or both groups at the same time. Another option would be to create two different inventory files, one for the canary group and the other for the main group with the groups having the same name so that variables are shared.

## Blue/Green deployment

**Blue/Green** deployment is very different from canary deployment and has some advantages and some disadvantages. The main advantages are:

- Easier to implement
- Allows quicker iterations
- All users get moved at the same time
- Rollbacks have no performance degradation

Among the disadvantages, the main ones are the fact that you need to have double the machines available than what your application requires. This disadvantage can be easily mitigated if the application is running on a cloud (either private, public, or hybrid) scaling up the application resources for the deployment and then scale them back down.

Implementing Blue/Green deployment in Ansible is very easy. The simplest way is to create two different inventories (one for blue and one for green) and then simply manage your infrastructure as if they are different environments such as production, staging, dev, and so on.

# Optimizations

Sometimes, Ansible feels slow, mainly if you have a very long list of tasks to execute and/or if you have huge amount of machines. This feeling is actually more than just a feeling. There are multiple reasons for this, and ways to avoid it, we are going to look at three of those.

## Pipelining

One of the reason why Ansible is slow by default is that for every module execution and for every host, Ansible will perform the following actions:

- SSH handshake
- Execute the task
- Close the SSH connection

As you can see, this means that if you have 10 tasks to be executed on a single remote server, Ansible will open (and close) the connection 10 times. Since the SSH protocol is an encrypted protocol, this makes the SSH handshake an even longer process, since the two parts have to negotiate the ciphers every single time.

Ansible allows us to reduce the execution time drastically by initiating the connections at the beginning of the playbook and keeping them alive for the whole execution so that it does not need to reopen the connection at every task. Over the course of Ansible life, this feature has changed name multiple times, as well as the way it's enabled. From version 1.5, it's been called **pipelining** and the way to enable it is by adding the following line to your `ansible.cfg` file:

```
pipelining=True
```

The reason why this feature is not enabled by default, is that many distributions ship with the `requiretty` option in `sudo`. The pipelining mode in Ansible and the `requiretty` option in `sudo` conflict and will make your playbooks fail.

> If you want to enable the pipelining mode, ensure that the `sudo` `requiretty` mode is disabled on your target machines.

## Optimizing with_items

If you want to execute similar operations multiple times, it's possible to repeat the same task multiple times with different parameters or use the `with_items` option. Aside from the fact that `with_items` makes your code easier to read and to follow, it could also improve your performance. An example is with the installation of packages (that is: `apt`, `dnf`, `yum`, `package` modules) where Ansible will perform a single command if you use `with_items` against a single command for each package if you don't. As you can imagine, this can help boosting your performance.

## Understanding what happens when your tasks are executed

Even after you implement the methods we just talked about to speed up the playbook execution, you may still find some tasks take a very long time. This is very common with some tasks, even if it's possible with many other modules. The modules that usually give you this problem are the following:

- Packaging management (that is: `apt`, `dnf`, `yum`, `package`)
- Cloud machine creation (that is: DigitalOcean, EC2)

The reason for this slowness is often non-Ansible specific. An example case could be if you used a packaging management module to update your machines. This requires downloading tens or hundreds of megabytes on every machine and installing a high quantity of software. A way to speed up this kind of operation is to have a local repository in your datacenter and have all your machines pointing to it instead of your distribution repositories. This will allow your machines to download at higher speed and without using the public connection that is often limited in bandwidth or metered.

It's often important to understand what the modules do in the background to optimize the playbook execution.

In the cloud machine creation case, Ansible just performs an API call to the chosen cloud provider and waits for the machine to be ready. DigitalOcean machines can take up to one minute to be created (and other clouds much longer) so Ansible will wait for that amount of time. Some modules have an asynchronous mode to avoid this wait period, but you'll have to ensure that the machine is ready before using it otherwise the modules that use the created machine will fail.

## Summary

In this chapter, we have seen how you can deploy an application with Ansible, as well as the various distribution and deployment strategies you can use. We also saw how to create RPM packages with Ansible and how to optimize the performance of Ansible using different methods.

In the last and final chapter, we will discuss Ansible on Windows, networking devices. Additionally, some Ansible Tower concepts will be discussed.

# 10
# Introducing Ansible for Enterprises

In this chapter, we will discuss the state of Ansible on different OSes. We'll also take a look at Ansible Galaxy and Ansible Tower.

We'll explore the following topics:

- Ansible on Windows
- Ansible for networking devices
- Ansible Galaxy
- Ansible Tower

## Ansible on Windows

Ansible version 1.7 started being able to manage Windows machines with a few basic modules. After the acquisition of Ansible by Red Hat, a lot of effort has been put into this task by Microsoft and many other companies and people. By the time of the 2.1 release, Ansible's ability to manage Windows machines was close to being complete. Some modules have been extended to work seamlessly on Unix and Windows, while in other cases, the Windows logic was so different from Unix that new modules needed to be created.

 At the moment, using Windows as a control machine is not supported, though some users have tweaked the code and their environment to make it work.

*Introducing Ansible for Enterprises*

The connection from the control machine to Windows machines is not made over SSH; instead, it's made over **Windows Remote Management (WinRM)**. You can visit Microsoft's website for a detailed explanation and implementation: `http://msdn.microsoft.com/en-us/library/aa384426(v=vs.85).aspx`.

On the control machine, once you've installed Ansible, it's important that you install WinRM. You can do it via `pip` with this command:

```
pip install "pywinrm>=0.1.1"
```

You may need to use `sudo` or the `root` account to execute this command.

On each of the remote Windows machines, you need to install PowerShell version 3.0 or higher. Ansible provides a couple of helpful scripts to set it up:

- **WinRM**: `https://github.com/ansible/ansible/blob/devel/examples/scripts/ConfigureRemotingForAnsible.ps1`
- **PowerShell 3.0 upgrade**: `https://github.com/cchurch/ansible/blob/devel/examples/scripts/upgrade_to_ps3.ps1`

You will also need to allow port `5986` via the firewall, as this is the default WinRM connection port, and make sure it is accessible from the command center.

To make sure you can access the service remotely, run a `curl` command:

```
curl -vk -d `` -u "$USER:$PASSWORD" "https://<IP>:5986/wsman".
```

If basic authentication works, you're set to start running commands. Once the setup is done, you're ready to start running Ansible! Let's run the equivalent of the Windows version of the `Hello, world!` program in Ansible by running `win_ping`. In order to do this, let's set up our credentials file.

This can be done using Ansible vault, as follows:

```
$ ansible-vault create group_vars/windows.yml
```

As we've seen, Ansible vault will ask interactively to set the password:

```
Vault password:
Confirm Vault password:
```

At this point, we can add the variables we need:

```
ansible_ssh_user: Administrator
ansible_ssh_pass: <password>
ansible_ssh_port: 5986
ansible_connection: winrm
```

Let's set up our inventory file, as follows:

```
[windows]
174.129.181.242
```

Followed by this, let's run `win_ping`:

**ansible windows -i inventory -m win_ping --ask-vault-pass**

Ansible will ask us the vault password and then print the result of the run, as follows:

```
Vault password:
174.129.181.242 | success >> {
    "changed": false,
    "ping": "pong"
}
```

# Ansible for networking devices

Since version 2.1, we have seen many new modules for the management of networking devices and softwares. Many of those modules have been contributed directly from the company that creates the device (or software). The big advantage of this, which is based on the idea of **Software Defined Networking** (**SDN**), is that having Ansible that manages all your networking infrastructure allows you to have an entire datacenter completely managed within Ansible. This means, having a single language for all components and all people within your IT, and this will allow people to understand better how the company IT works as well as working more closely with each other.

# Ansible Galaxy

Ansible Galaxy is a free site from where you can download Ansible roles developed by the community and kick-start your automation within minutes. You can share or review community roles so that others can easily find the most trusted roles on Ansible Galaxy. You can start using Ansible Galaxy by simply signing up with social media applications such as Twitter, Google, and GitHub or by creating a new account on the Ansible Galaxy website at `https://galaxy.ansible.com/` and downloading the required roles using the `ansible-galaxy` command, which ships with Ansible version 1.4.2 and higher.

> In case you want to host your own local Ansible Galaxy instance, you can do so by fetching the code from `https://github.com/ansible/galaxy`.

To download an Ansible role from Ansible Galaxy, use the following syntax:

```
ansible-galaxy install username.rolename
```

You can also specify a version as follows:

```
ansible-galaxy install username.rolename[,version]
```

If you don't specify a version, then the `ansible-galaxy` command will download the latest available version. You can install multiple roles in two ways; firstly, by passing multiple role names separated by a space, as follows:

```
ansible-galaxy install username.rolename[,version] username.rolename[,version]
```

Secondly, you can do so by specifying role names in a file and passing that filename to the `-r`/`--role-file` option. For instance, you could create the `requirements.txt` file with the following content:

```
user1.rolename,v1.0.0
user2.rolename,v1.1.0
user3.rolename,v1.2.1
```

You could then install roles by passing the filename to the `ansible-galaxy` command, as follows:

```
ansible-galaxy install -r requirements
```

Let's see how you can use `ansible-galaxy` to download a role for Apache HTTPd:

```
sudo ansible-galaxy install geerlingguy.apache
```

You'll see output like this:

```
- downloading role 'apache', owned by geerlingguy
- downloading role from
https://github.com/geerlingguy/ansible-role-apache/archive/1.7.3.tar.gz
- extracting geerlingguy.apache to
/etc/ansible/roles/geerlingguy.apache
- geerlingguy.apache was installed successfully
```

The preceding `ansible-galaxy` command will download the Apache HTTPd role to the `/etc/ansible/roles` directory. You can now directly use the preceding role in your playbook, creating the `playbooks/galaxy.yaml` file with the following content:

```
- hosts: web
  user: ansible
  become: True
  roles:
  - geerlingguy.apache
```

As you can see, we created a simple playbook with a `geerlingguy.apache` role. We can now test it:

```
ansible-playbook playbooks/galaxy.yaml
```

This should give us the following output:

```
PLAY [web] ************************************************************

TASK [setup] **********************************************************
ok: [ws01.fale.io]
ok: [ws02.fale.io]

TASK [geerlingguy.apache : Include OS-specific variables.] *******
ok: [ws01.fale.io]
ok: [ws02.fale.io]

TASK [geerlingguy.apache : Define apache_packages.] *************
ok: [ws01.fale.io]
ok: [ws02.fale.io]

TASK [geerlingguy.apache : Ensure Apache is installed on RHEL.] **
changed: [ws01.fale.io] => (item=[u'httpd', u'httpd-devel', u'mod_ssl', u'openssh'])
changed: [ws02.fale.io] => (item=[u'httpd', u'httpd-devel', u'mod_ssl',
```

```
u'openssh'])

    TASK [geerlingguy.apache : Ensure Apache is installed on Suse.] **
    skipping: [ws01.fale.io] => (item=[])
    skipping: [ws02.fale.io] => (item=[])

    TASK [geerlingguy.apache : Update apt cache.] *******************
    skipping: [ws01.fale.io]
    skipping: [ws02.fale.io]

    TASK [geerlingguy.apache : Ensure Apache is installed on Debian.]
    skipping: [ws01.fale.io] => (item=[])
    skipping: [ws02.fale.io] => (item=[])

    TASK [geerlingguy.apache : Ensure Apache is installed on Solaris.]
    skipping: [ws01.fale.io] => (item=httpd)
    skipping: [ws02.fale.io] => (item=httpd)
    skipping: [ws01.fale.io] => (item=httpd-devel)
    skipping: [ws02.fale.io] => (item=httpd-devel)
    skipping: [ws02.fale.io] => (item=mod_ssl)
    skipping: [ws01.fale.io] => (item=mod_ssl)
    skipping: [ws02.fale.io] => (item=openssh)
    skipping: [ws01.fale.io] => (item=openssh)

    TASK [geerlingguy.apache : Get installed version of Apache.] *****
    ok: [ws01.fale.io]
    ok: [ws02.fale.io]

    TASK [geerlingguy.apache : Create apache_version variable.] ******
    ok: [ws01.fale.io]
    ok: [ws02.fale.io]

    TASK [geerlingguy.apache : include_vars] ************************
    skipping: [ws01.fale.io]
    skipping: [ws02.fale.io]

    TASK [geerlingguy.apache : include_vars] ************************
    ok: [ws01.fale.io]
    ok: [ws02.fale.io]

    TASK [geerlingguy.apache : Configure Apache.] *******************
    ok: [ws01.fale.io] => (item={u'regexp': u'^Listen ', u'line': u'Listen 80'})
    ok: [ws02.fale.io] => (item={u'regexp': u'^Listen ', u'line': u'Listen 80'})

    TASK [geerlingguy.apache : Check whether certificates defined in vhosts exist.]
```

```
    TASK [geerlingguy.apache : Add apache vhosts configuration.] *****
    changed: [ws01.fale.io]
    changed: [ws02.fale.io]

    TASK [geerlingguy.apache : Configure Apache.] ********************
    skipping: [ws01.fale.io] => (item={u'regexp': u'^Listen ', u'line':
u'Listen 80'})
    skipping: [ws02.fale.io] => (item={u'regexp': u'^Listen ', u'line':
u'Listen 80'})

    TASK [geerlingguy.apache : Check whether certificates defined in vhosts
exist.]

    TASK [geerlingguy.apache : Add apache vhosts configuration.] *****
    skipping: [ws01.fale.io]
    skipping: [ws02.fale.io]

    TASK [geerlingguy.apache : Configure Apache.] ********************
    skipping: [ws01.fale.io] => (item={u'regexp': u'^Listen ', u'line':
u'Listen 80'})
    skipping: [ws02.fale.io] => (item={u'regexp': u'^Listen ', u'line':
u'Listen 80'})

    TASK [geerlingguy.apache : Enable Apache mods.] ******************
    skipping: [ws01.fale.io] => (item=rewrite.load)
    skipping: [ws02.fale.io] => (item=rewrite.load)
    skipping: [ws01.fale.io] => (item=ssl.load)
    skipping: [ws02.fale.io] => (item=ssl.load)

    TASK [geerlingguy.apache : Disable Apache mods.] *****************

    TASK [geerlingguy.apache : Check whether certificates defined in vhosts
exist.]

    TASK [geerlingguy.apache : Add apache vhosts configuration.] *****
    skipping: [ws01.fale.io]
    skipping: [ws02.fale.io]

    TASK [geerlingguy.apache : Add vhost symlink in sites-enabled.] **
    skipping: [ws01.fale.io]
    skipping: [ws02.fale.io]

    TASK [geerlingguy.apache : Remove default vhost in sites-enabled.]
    skipping: [ws01.fale.io]
    skipping: [ws02.fale.io]

    TASK [geerlingguy.apache : Configure Apache.] ********************
    skipping: [ws01.fale.io] => (item={u'regexp': u'^Listen ', u'line':
```

# Introducing Ansible for Enterprises

```
u'Listen 80'})
    skipping: [ws02.fale.io] => (item={u'regexp': u'^Listen ', u'line':
u'Listen 80'})

    TASK [geerlingguy.apache : Add apache vhosts configuration.] *****
    skipping: [ws01.fale.io]
    skipping: [ws02.fale.io]

    TASK [geerlingguy.apache : Ensure Apache has selected state and enabled
on boot.]
    ok: [ws01.fale.io]
    ok: [ws02.fale.io]

    RUNNING HANDLER [geerlingguy.apache : restart apache] ************
    changed: [ws01.fale.io]
    changed: [ws02.fale.io]

    PLAY RECAP ***********************************************************
    ws01.fale.io         : ok=11    changed=3    unreachable=0    failed=0
    ws02.fale.io         : ok=11    changed=3    unreachable=0    failed=0
```

As you may have noticed, many steps were skipped due to the fact that this role is designed to work on many different Linux distributions.

# Ansible Tower

Ansible Tower is a web-based GUI developed by Red Hat. Ansible Tower provides you with an easy-to-use dashboard to manage your nodes and role-based authentication to control access to your Ansible Tower dashboard. The biggest features of Ansible Tower are as follows:

- **LDAP/AD integration**: You can import (and give privileges to) users based on the result of LDAP/AD queries that Ansible Tower performs on your LDAP/AD server
- **Role-based access control**: Limit the users to only run the playbooks they are authorized to run and/or target only a limited amount of hosts

- **REST API**: All Ansible Tower capabilities are exposed via a REST API
- **Job scheduling**: Ansible Tower allows us to schedule jobs (playbook execution)
- **Graphical inventory management**: Ansible Tower manages the inventory in a more dynamic way than Ansible
- **Dashboard**: Ansible Tower allows us to see the situation of all current and previous job executions
- **Logging**: Ansible Tower logs all the results of every job execution to be able to go back and check if needed

Although Red Hat has promised to make Ansible Tower open source soon, at the moment, it is not freely available and you need to pay depending on the number of nodes you want to manage.

At the time of writing, Red Hat provides a free copy of Ansible Tower for 10 nodes. For more details, visit the Ansible Tower website at `http://www.ansible.com/tower`; the user guide is available at `http://docs.ansible.com/ansible-tower/`.

# Summary

In this chapter, we have seen some options that Ansible and its ecosystem provide us. This chapter also wants to teach you to search even less canonical things on the Ansible documentation, because it could be that Ansible has such capability. Also, as you may have noticed, in this chapter many of the covered topics have had major changes in 2.1 (released less than 6 months before the publication of the second edition of this book) and are very actively developed areas, so the official documentation is the right place to check the current state of such topics.

# Index

**--**

--skip-tags 190

## A

agent-based systems
  about 11, 12
  agent component 12
  server component 12
  versus agent-less systems 12
agent-less systems 12
Amazon lambda functions 151
Amazon Simple Notification Service (SNS) 152, 153
  about 151
  messages 151
  publishers 151
  subscribers 151
  topics 151
Amazon Simple Queue Service (SQS) 151
Amazon Web Services (AWS) 119
  about 70, 121
  account, setting up 125, 126
  aws_access_key 152
  aws_secret_key 152
  complex deployment 134
  Elastic Block Storage (EBS) 124
  Elastic Compute Cloud (EC2) 123
  global infrastructure 122
  Identity and Access Management 125
  region 152
  relational database service 125
  Route 53 124
  simple deployment 127, 129
  simple storage service 122
  Virtual Private Cloud (VPC) 123, 124
Ansible Galaxy 240, 241
  URL 240
Ansible Tower 244
  dashboard 245
  graphical inventory management 245
  job scheduling 245
  LDAP / AD integration 244
  logging 245
  references 245
  REST API 245
  role-based access control 244
Ansible
  about 13, 28, 29, 30
  audit trail 119
  determining 13, 14
  for networking devices 239
  functional testing 186
  installing 14
  installing, from source 16, 17, 18
  installing, system's package manager used 15
  installing, via Apt 15
  installing, via Homebrew 15
  installing, via pip 16
  installing, via Yum 15
  iterates, working 72
  moving servers 119
  multiple staging environments 119
  on Windows 237, 238, 239
  references 238
  URL, for downloading 70
  used, with Git 24, 25
  user, creating 48, 49
  vault, used 110, 111, 112
  verbosity 37
Apache Subversion (SVN) 23
assert
  using, for functional testing 186, 187
attach parameter 145

Availability Zones (AZ) 122

## B

bash modules
  using 168
basic server
  configuring 49
  EPEL, enabling 49
  FirewallD, enabled 52
  hostname, changing 54
  installed packages, upgrading 50, 51
  MOTD, adding 53
  NTP, configuring 51
  NTP, executing 51
  NTP, installed 51
  playbook, executing 56
  playbook, reviewing 54
  Python bindings, installing for SELinux 50
blue deployment
  about 233
  advantages 233
Boolean value 87, 88

## C

canary deployment
  about 232
  advantages 232
CentOS cloud image
  reference link 19
check mode 181, 182
compiled software
  building, with RPM packaging 226, 230
Concurrent Versions System (CVS) 23
conditionals 60
  Boolean value 87, 88
  Jinja2 filters, used 108
  variable, checking 89
  working 85, 87
configuration parameters
  ansible__type 69
  ansible_connection 69
  ansible_host 69
  ansible_port 69
  ansible_private_key_file 69
  ansible_user 69

overriding, with inventory file 68
Continuous Integration (CI) 179
Create, Remove, Update, or Delete (CRUD)
  operation 35
cycles 61

## D

data
  formatting, Jinja2 filters used 107
deployment strategies
  about 231, 232
  blue deployment 233
  canary deployment 232
  green deployment 233
DigitalOcean
  about 71, 135, 136
  advantages 135, 136
  deployment in 138
  droplets 136
  private networking 137
  SSH key management 136
  SSH key, adding in 137
DNS as a Service (DNSaaS) 124
Don't Repeat Yourself (DRY) principle 89
droplets 136
dynamic inventory 63
  Amazon Web Services (AWS) 70, 71
  DigitalOcean 71
  working 69, 70

## E

e-mails 144, 145
EC2 Classic 123
Elastic Block Storage (EBS) 124
Elastic Compute Cloud (EC2) 123
environment
  preparing 206, 210
EPEL
  enabling 49
exceptions
  managing 190, 192
execution strategies 105
  free execution 106
  linear execution 105
  serial execution 105

exit_json
  working 165, 167

## F

fail_json
  working 165, 167
fileglobs loop - with_fileglobs 76
files
  copying, from local machine 204
  using, differences indicating 183
filters 60
FirewallD
  enabled 52
Fully Qualified Domain Name (FQDN) 28
functional testing 186
  Ansible 186
  assert, used 186, 187

## G

Git branch
  code based 198
Git
  Ansible, used 24, 25
global infrastructure 122
  Availability Zones (AZ) 122
  edge location 122
  region 122
green deployment
  about 233
  advantages 233
group variables 67

## H

handlers
  working 90
host variables 67
hostname
  changing 54
hosts 64

## I

Identity and Access Management
  about 125
  features 125

include
  working 89, 90
Information and Communication Technology (ICT)
  field 203
Infrastructure as a Service (IaaS) 120
Initialization (INI) format 63
installed packages
  upgrading 50, 51
integer loop - with_sequence 77
Internet Relay Chat (IRC) 149
  channel 150
  color 150
  msg 150
  nick 150
  port 150
  server 150
  style 150
  use_ssl 150
inventory file 64
  configuration parameters, overriding with 68
  groups in 64
  regular expressions in 66
  working 63
inventory variable files 68
IT automation
  about 8
  advantages 8
  agent-based systems 11
  agent-based systems, versus agent-less systems 12
  agent-less systems 12
  disadvantages 9
  error propagation, damages limiting 9, 10, 11
  history 8
  types 11
iterates
  fileglobs loop - with_fileglobs 76
  integer loop - with_sequence 77
  nested loops - with_nested 74
  standard iteration - with_items 73
  working, in Ansible 72

## J

Jinja2 60
Jinja2 templates

conditionals 61
cycles 61
Jinja2
  filters 60, 107
  templates 60
  undefined variables, defaulting 109, 110
  used, for data formatting 107
  used, with conditionals 108
  variables 60
Jinja
  filters 106

# K

Keep It Simple Stupid (KISS) principle 36
Kernel Virtual Machine (KVM) 136
Kernel-based Virtual Machine (KVM) 18, 28
key-value format 157

# L

Lightweight Resources and Providers (LWRPs) 158
local_action feature
  working 82, 83
loops
  reference link 79

# M

mail module
  attach parameter 145
  port parameter 145
Masterless Puppet 12
module 30
  testing 174, 176, 177

# N

n_log
  using 116
Nagios 153
nested loops - with_nested 74
networking devices
  Ansible 239
NTP
  configuring 51
  executing 51
  installed 51

# O

optimization 234
  pipelining 234
  tasks, executed 235
  with_items, optimizing 235

# P

passwords
  hiding 115, 116
pipelining 234
playbooks 113
  anatomy, studying 30, 32
  executing 32, 33, 34, 35, 36, 54, 56
  handlers, in role 102, 105
  helper files 98, 101
  reviewing 54, 56
  transforming, in Ansible 94
  transforming, in role 95, 97
  variables in 38, 39, 40, 46
  webserver role, transforming 101, 102
  working 30
port parameter 145
PowerShell 3.0 upgrade
  reference link 238
Preboot Execution Environment (PXE) 157
private domain 126
private networking 137
project organization 93, 94
public domain 126
Python bindings
  installing, for SELinux 50
Python modules
  exit_json, working 165, 167
  fail_json, working 165, 167
  testing 167
  using 159, 164

# Q

Quality Assurance (QA) process 186
Quick Emulator (QEMU) 18

## R

relational database service 125
resources
  Complex Amazon Web Service deployment 121
  Digital Ocean 121
  Docker 121
  provisioning, in cloud 120
  Simple Amazon Web Service deployment 121
revision control system (RCS) 23
revision control system
  disadvantages 205
  web app, deploying with 211, 212
  with branches 204, 205
  with tags 205
Rocket Chat 148
roles
  anatomy 94
  playbooks, transforming in Ansible 95
  project organization 93, 94
  working 93
Route 53 124
RPM packages 206
  building 217
  building, with Ansible 219, 222, 223, 225
  building, with CI/CD pipeline 226
  Specifics (Spec) file, creating 214, 216, 217
  web app, deploying with 214
Ruby modules
  using 170, 172

## S

Secure Shell (SSH) 13
security groups 127
security management
  about 110
  Ansible, vault used 110, 111, 112
  n_log, used 116
  passwords, hiding 115, 116
  playbooks 113
  user passwords, encrypting 114
  vaults 113
SELinux
  Python bindings, installing 50
Serverless Chef 12

setup_apache.yaml file
  example 31
  hosts 31
  remote_user 31
  tasks 31
sh shell 69
simple storage service
  about 122
  price schema 123
  reliability 123
  tooling 123
Slack 147, 148
software distribution strategy
  about 203, 204
  files, copying from local machine 204
  revision control system, with branches 204, 205
  revision control system, with tags 205
  RPM packages 206
Source Code Control System (SCCS) 23
Specifics (Spec) file
  about 214
  creating 214, 216, 217
SSH key management 136
stable branch
  with multiple folders 198, 200
standard iteration - with_items 73
stream editor (sed) 49

## T

tags
  testing 188
task
  delegating 83
tasks blocks 106
template task 94
test environment
  creating, with KVM 18, 19, 21
  creating, with QEMU 18, 19, 21
trigger failure 194

## U

undefined variables
  defaulting 109, 110
user passwords
  encrypting 114

# V

variable
  checking 89
variables 60
  group variables 67
  host variables 67
  inventory variable files 68
  working 66
vaults 113
verbose (-v) option 37
verbose mode 176
version control system 22, 23
  advantages 22
Virtual Private Cloud (VPC) 123, 124

# W

web app

deploying, with revision control system 211, 212
deploying, with RPM packages 214
web server
  configuring 57
  installing 57
website
  publishing 59
Windows Remote Management (WinRM) 238
  reference link 238
Windows
  Ansible on 237, 238, 239

# X

XMPP 146

# Y

YAML Ain't Markup Language (YAML) 27, 28

CPSIA information can be obtained
at www.ICGtesting.com
Printed in the USA
FSHW02n1319171018
53088FS